PRAISE FOR *MISFIT*

D1003829

"In *Misfit to Masterpiece*, Dr. Diane Pearce has fashioned a resource which should be read by anyone bearing deep emotional wounds. Not only does Diane 'demystify' the process of healing in order to help travelers see the end from the beginning, she also gives readers an insider's glimpse into the miracle of her own healing journey. The result is breathtaking and the hope is palpable!"

REV. MICHAEL JOHN CUSICK, M.A., L.P.C.
Author of *Surfing for God*
President and Founder of Restoring the Soul Ministries

"*Misfit to Masterpiece* will prove to be a necessary handbook for doing life! I bought a copy for several family members and friends and I have become addicted to my copy! A must read for all walks of life and all stages of grace!"

DEB COPELAND, Founder & Servant, Live to Give…A GOD Thing
Bestselling Author of *Attitude Therapy*
Good Morning… Good Night - 99 Days to Your Spiritual Recovery
and Co-author of *Face to Face with God - Healing the Cry Within*

"I have been deeply inspired by Dr Diane Pearce's courage to face the pain of her life, embrace the truth of healing love, and dedicate herself to helping others experience the same. She has truly redefined herself in a life-long application of spiritual remediation, and then shared the details of this process in *Misfit to Masterpiece* for all to benefit."

JIM VIGORITO, Ph.D., Licensed Psychologist, Hawaii

"Viktor E. Frankl made the observation that 'The one thing you can't take away from me is the way I choose to respond to what you do to me. The last of one's freedoms is to choose one's attitude in any given circumstance.'

Diane Pearce chose her response and her attitude, and since that day she has proven to be a skillful guide in helping hurting people find their way. Diane's personal journey gives her a depth of wisdom few people have to assist others in finding the healing they desperately need. It is one thing to 'tell your story' but something vastly greater is required to 'live your story.' Diane has lived her story and now through *Misfit to Masterpiece* she can help you write a new chapter of healing in your life.

For twenty years she has been my friend, my confidant and my 'go-to' counselor when I have people who require expertise in getting past their past. This book will bless all those who are hurting as well as those who bring hope to the hurting."

DR. DWIGHT "IKE" REIGHARD
President/CEO, MUST Ministries
Senior Pastor, Piedmont Church

Misfit
to
Masterpiece

Uncover the Secrets to Changing Your Legacy

by M. Diane Pearce

Misfit to Masterpiece

Copyright © 2014 by M. Diane Pearce

Published by
Legacy Strategy Publishing, 1815 Old 41 Hwy., Suite 110, Kennesaw, GA 30152
678-468-9103
Visit www.legacystrategy.com

Cover Design: Tim Pearce

Interior Design: Monica Hardy

ISBN: 978-0-9904422-0-2

ISBN: 978-0-9904422-1-9

Printed and bound in the United States of America

"If your law had not been my delight,
I would have perished in my affliction."
Psalm 119:92

Table of Contents

Chapter 1: A Heart of Stone in the Making.................................... 3

Chapter 2: Transformation Continues! 11

Chapter 3: The Heart's Path of Healing and Recovery..................... 15

Chapter 4: Your Journey of Transformation.................................... 19

Chapter 5: Strategies for Using God's Word 23

Chapter 6: Strategies for Repairing the Heart 31

Chapter 7: Strategies for Healing the Hurt 45

Biblical Strategies for Healing My Legacy

My Significance... 59

My Security... 60

My Stability.. 61

My Abandonment... 62

My Angels 63

My Anger.. 63

My Attitude 64

My Battle.. 65

My Balance 66

My Beauty... 67

My Body 68

My Bondage.. 69

My Boundaries.. 70

My Calling... 70

My Child 72

My Comfort 74

My Communication with Others 75

My Confidence 76

My Critics 77

My Defender 78

My Delivery 79

My Despair 79

My Dignity 80

My Discipline 81

My Disappointments 82

My Enemies 82

My Faith 84

My Family 85

My Fears 86

My Friendships 87

My God 88

My Grief 89

My Guardrails 89

My Guide 90

My Guilt 91

My Happiness 92

My Healing 93

My Heart 93

My Help 95

My Hope 96

My Humility 98

My Hurt 98

My Identity 100

My Integrity 101

My Jealousy 101

My Justice 102

My Legacy 104

My Marriage 105

My Mentoring 106

My Mercy 107

My Money 107

My Mouth 108

My Obstacles 109

My Parent 109

My Path 110

My Peace 112

My Place 112

My Prayers 114

My Pride 115

My Prison 117

My Protection 117

My Purpose 118

My Refuge 120

My Relationships 121

My Repentance 121

My Safety 123

My Sin 123

My Strength 125

My Transformation 126
My Trust 127
My Victory 128
My Waiting 129
My Walk 130
My Wisdom 131
My Work 132
My Worship 133
My Wounds 134

I am Forever Grateful for...

Paul E. Winegardner (1924-1998),
A courageous man who taught me that our Maker's
design for us is to bring Him honor from how we live.

Barbara Winegardner,
A woman of courage.

Dan & Jenna Houmes,
For mentoring me with tenacity.

Rev. Charles & Isabelle Pearce,
For their example of mercy towards others.

Donna Gillespie,
For her untiring patience with me
throughout this book.

Tim Pearce,
My best friend who has taught
me how to laugh.

"The means of the blessing may change
but the source never changes!"
Rev. Charles Pearce, August 21, 1983

INTRODUCTION

For every person who reads this and has been abandoned, neglected or abused, this is written for you. You may have been hurt and perhaps deeply wounded by others, possibly even by your own decisions and choices. No matter how discarded you may feel, your Creator sees your hurt like no one else. I am evidence that there is hope for each and every one of us, even when all hope seems lost. God also sees your potential like no one else! I know because He saw my potential when I had no reason to have any hope at all.

When we are hurt, we have choices. We can withdraw, lash out at others, or even worse, pretend we were not hurt at all. The result of these choices is always harmful. Another option is to allow our hurt to be healed by the Creator of our soul! For this to happen, **it is essential that the healing penetrate as deeply as the wounds that have been left behind.**

I invite you into my own deep place of healing and transformation. My wounds were deep; therefore, transformation was needed deep within me. My scars remind me that without the healing of my

Creator **I would be nothing**, and so I will be forever grateful to Him. Because of Jesus Christ, I am somebody with a purpose of divine appointment. Without Him, I would be nothing more than a statistic.

Before you proceed, keep in mind that I am thankful for each of the events that you are about to read. I am thankful because each of them have contributed something to who I am today, a masterpiece of God's making. So, do not allow yourself to ask "Why?" I spent enough time on that question before I was able to finally say to God, "Why not me? Thank you for the events that left me a misfit as well as for the pain that they brought. For without those things happening in my life, I would not be a masterpiece who brings you honor and glory."

Chapter 1

A Heart of Stone in the Making

Fresh bruises formed under her skin, and angry tears stung her eyes as 16 year-old Marilyn ran to the window in the small, mice-infested attic that served as her bedroom. She threw open the window, reached outside, and grabbed the clothes she had hung there the previous night.

She quickly folded the outfit and placed it on top of her Bible and a pair of shoes already in the brown paper bag that served as her luggage. She ran down the steep attic stairs and through the kitchen leading to the back door. For a brief moment, Marilyn took one last look through tear-filled eyes at the place she had called home.

With one hand clutching the door, and the other holding tightly to the paper bag containing the few possessions she felt she couldn't live without, Marilyn yelled to whoever might be listening, "I'm leaving!" She then turned the knob, opened the door, and walked out of the house - out of the house and away from the only parents she could remember. Out of the house into a future she could never have imagined.

By the time Marilyn reached the road in front of her house, the school buses had completed their Friday morning routes and were parked and waiting for the school day to end. A farmer on his way into town to pick up supplies stopped and picked up the teenage girl hitchhiking on the side of the road. His first look at her told him she was very upset and most likely in some sort of trouble. When she told him her destination, he didn't hesitate to take her to the place she requested.

A Runaway Girl

The farmer was polite with kind eyes and he told her "good luck" as they arrived at the local police station. Marilyn felt terribly self-conscious and hesitated for a moment. Then, with gritted teeth, she walked up the steps into the station. She was nervous and embarrassed, but determined. So when the police officer asked what was going on, Marilyn told all. She told him that she had run away from home and that she wasn't going back. She told him that if he made her go back, she'd run away again, and again, and again, no matter how many times it took. She was indignant. She would not stay in that house.

Law enforcement quickly made the decision to involve Social Services. Marilyn was escorted across the street to another government office where another man sitting behind another desk asked her more questions and asked for more details.

As she dug deep for the strength she needed, she silently prayed. She prayed for the courage to speak and to tell it all. She was afraid but determination outweighed the fear. Mr. Smith, the Social Services worker that interviewed Marilyn, was especially gentle with her. His manner gave her a sense of safety she could not remember ever feeling. From somewhere deep inside her came the courage and the strength she needed to tell him her story - everything no matter what the outcome might be.

There were times while relating the horrific events that his eyes filled with tears. She feared that he didn't believe her, but when he asked to see her bruises and Marilyn reluctantly rolled up her dirty long sleeves and pant legs that revealed the evidence of numerous beatings, Mr. Smith's emotions seemed to overwhelm him.

The tenderness was not only apparent in his eyes but in his voice as well and for the first time in a long while Marilyn allowed herself to relax a little. She no longer carried such an ugly secret, alone. The relief she felt at that moment overwhelmed her causing her to cry and yet smile at the same time. With terrible secrets expelled, she began to feel a peaceful calm that was unexplainable.

By the end of that beautiful spring Friday in 1977, Marilyn's living nightmare had ended with the help of Mr. Smith. And though she didn't know it yet, something even better had begun. Though Marilyn was now homeless for the second time in her life, God was working to pave a new path that would begin the process of healing!

An Orphaned Girl

A year earlier in the spring of 1976, Marilyn's home life had gone from hopeful to hopeless. Marilyn had been adopted in 1965. What orphaned child wouldn't want to be adopted? However, her adoptive parents had begun telling her she should appreciate them for what they did for her and how much she owed them for taking her in when no one wanted her. Soon they required Marilyn to "pay them back for all they had done for her."

The pay back included tolerating and keeping the secret of her daily verbal and physical abuse, which included withholding food and forbidding personal hygiene. Marilyn was eventually put in charge of feeding and cleaning up after the 120 Pomeranian dogs that the couple raised inside the house. This was in addition to the 20 cats living in one room, as well as any chickens from their backyard chicken farm that had gotten sick. The sick chickens were kept in the attic, which also served as Marilyn's bedroom. Furthermore, during the winter months, the home was infested with mice. At the time, Marilyn assumed that this was normal, and she should not question anything that occurred in this house.

A Girl called "Dog"

At school, Marilyn's nickname was "Dog." Being around her for just a few seconds was enough to explain why—she smelled like the dogs she cleaned up after. Her mother explained that they had to conserve water, so 16 year-old Marilyn was on water rations for laundry and bathing. She was told that she was a problem child that no one wanted. Given that they had been kind enough to take her in, it would have been ungrateful of her to question their decisions.

A typical day would start at 5:00 am when Marilyn's mother would wake her to start chores. Her mother would return to bed while Marilyn got the animals taken care of for the start of the day. Marilyn's work would have to pass inspection before she was allowed to go to school. However, not passing inspection didn't just mean missing school; it also meant physical and verbal abuse, as well as starvation.

This was Marilyn's morning routine for three years with the exception of Friday through Sunday. School was not allowed on Friday because that was the day designated by her mother to stay home and work with the animals.

When Marilyn became an adolescent, the abuse took a more severe turn which threw her into a deeper state of confusion. This confusion and trauma began a new phase for her - something snapped and she began to fight back. Although her mother's obsessive drinking, the degrading living conditions, and abusive behavior had prompted her to a deeper level of despair, Marilyn's life was about to change for the good but it had to hit rock bottom first.

A Girl on the Brink of Suicide

In the spring of 1976, Marilyn decided to end her pain by ending her life. She concluded in her despair that living had become hopeless. She was tired of fighting so hard just to merely survive and her heart was numbed to the point that she had no hope for the future and no feelings left for herself. Marilyn was cold and empty, and she was tired of stealing food and working to be invisible in order to survive. Because she always had an odor about her on the school bus, Marilyn was not allowed by the other students to sit in a seat like everyone else. Instead, she sat on the steps just inside the bus door. The plan to end her life was simple enough, or so she thought. One day Marilyn decided that she would wait until the bus was at a good speed in traffic then she would jump up, push open the doors, and leap into oncoming traffic to her death.

However, by the time she had worked up the courage to follow through, the bus had arrived at school. Marilyn decided she would do what it took to survive one more day at school and then follow through on her plan that afternoon on the way home. But, by the end of that school day, a student named Leah came and spoke truth to Marilyn—a truth that changed her life forever. Leah said to Marilyn, "I know that no one likes you, and you don't have any friends. But, I know someone who loves you - loves you enough to give his life for you!" Upon hearing these words of truth, Marilyn accepted Christ's love for her. For the first time that she could remember, she felt like **she** was valuable. If God loved her so much that He would allow His Son to die on the cross for her sins, then she must be important to **Him**. Upon accepting His love for her, she got onto her school bus that afternoon a changed person. She no longer wanted to take her life. Instead, Marilyn's cold heart of stone had a **purpose for living**!

A Girl with Angels at Her Side

Marilyn decided that since she was important to someone, she deserved to sit on a seat of the school bus like the other students. With the confidence that one gets when having the **strength of angels present and guarding her every step**, she took a seat and never again sat on the steps of the bus.

Shortly after this seemingly small courageous step of sitting on the seat in that bus, Marilyn began to pray. She prayed earnestly that God would be merciful towards her and allow her family to know God the way that she knew Him. She prayed with a child-like faith and fully believed that her family would change. After praying this daily for almost a solid year, her prayers were answered in a way that she never thought possible.

Upon realizing that she could have a real relationship with a God that she could not see with her eyes but yet feel His strong daily presence, she began to make a few friends at school. One of those students who also had a similar relationship with God was Beth.

Beth had a particularly kind and gentle way about her. She recognized Marilyn as a troubled and lonely teen who desperately needed love. Beth and her sister Marti were both teens who walked in faith because of their parents' example of living a life that was dedicated to God. They invited Marilyn to go to church on Sundays. She accepted their invites every single time even though she was severely punished by her adopted parents each time she went.

Marilyn began to use Beth's parents in her prayers as an example of what she wanted her own family to be like. Her prayers were heartfelt and desperate. Marilyn did not believe that she would live much longer if her adoptive parents did not change. She prayed believing that her family would become like this family of four that loved God and wanted to please Him with the way that they treated each other. Her prayers were answered but not in the way that had expected.

After Marilyn disclosed to Mr. Smith the events that led her to decide to run away on that spring morning in 1977, he took her back to school with the assurance that he would find somewhere safe for her to sleep that night. Though she knew she was homeless, she tried to go through her school day as normally as she could. Mr. Smith had given her a lunch pass and she was looking forward to eating all the hot cafeteria food that her tummy would allow. However, God had bigger plans for her than a hot lunch could provide!

Due to the plans that God had already put in place and the obedience and mercy of Beth's family, by the end of that school day, Marilyn was invited into their home to spend the weekend! Then the invite was extended to stay for a week, then for a month, and then the invitation was extended to stay with them...permanently! God had answered her prayer in a way that no one could have imagined possible. She did nothing to bring this to pass but pray and obey his promptings for her to act when she was in danger.

Looking back, the decision to believe in God's love for her and sit on those bus seats in 1976 began a series of decisions which reflected that she believed in God and the value that He sees when He looks at each of us as His creation!

The changes she made started with hearing truth and **making choices based on that truth!** Marilyn began to make choices that reflected the truth instead of making choices that reflected her emotions. Choices that have required her to **take every thought captive** and to make each **thought** obedient to Christ and His truth (2 Corinthians 10:5).

Chapter 2

Transformation Continues!

Though I began my life as Marilyn, a child abandoned by her incapable birth parents, abused by her adoptive parents, and embraced by a loving family at the age of 16, in 1976, a deep transformation began to take place inside of me. Over the next eight years my wounds began to heal as I experienced the love of a family and a consistent learning environment.

Since 1984, it has been my turn to help others. Guiding others through the steps of overcoming their past has become a divinely appointed purpose. Being married since 1987, and a mother since 1993, I have spoken across the Southeast sharing my story. It has been a blessing to encourage people to see that **"No one who has been a victim must remain a victim!"** I am living proof that there is a way to overcome horrific obstacles, to rebuild a self-esteem that has been reduced to nothing through life's circumstances, and to go on to fulfill God's purpose for your life.

Capable Hands

My heart was restored and continues to transform due to being in very capable hands. If I could begin to change at the age of 15 with my limited resources, then I believe anyone can change. However, I will be the first to tell you that I didn't do it alone. Just as all victims of childhood abuse and neglect need help, I had to have help too. My road to healing and recovery was orchestrated by God through His word and through people who were willing to listen to Him and provide assistance to me. I was in God's hands, because prior to the age of 16 I had no one who had been willing to treasure me as their own. I have found that God's hands are the only hands that are fully capable of caring for me the way I need.

Moving from a path of brokenness to a path of healing and recovery requires us to lean into the Master's hands. We must be willing to do our part, yield, and learn to trust Him so that He can finely tune our hearts to reflect His glory and the beauty He created within each and every one of us.

Because of my past, I had the potential to become a tough, cold woman with a bitter heart! It would have been easy for me to become a woman with a heart of stone who was relentless in outrunning the past. Without the **Truth**, I may have become the social recluse that was afraid of everyone around her and, therefore, never venturing out of my comfort zone. I could have chosen to isolate myself and remain safely hidden away from all potential hurts.

Never Forgotten

Instead, I worked at choosing to surrender to God's hands and not remain in the care of my own hands. I hope you will choose to entrust yourself to His very capable hands. His hands are not only capable but they are also the very hands that we are engraved upon! **We are engraved on His hands** because He values us as His very own creation! "Though a mother may forget you, I will not forget you! See, I have engraved you on the palms of my hands." Isaiah 49:15b-16. **Can you entrust your heart to the One who values you this much?** I made the most important choice in my life when I chose to trust Him more than I trust myself. It turned out to be a very wise choice for me; although, I did not know at the time how very significant it would turn out to be. Won't you join me on the exciting journey of continued trust and into complete recovery?

Chapter 3

The Heart's Path of Healing and Recovery

It took years of faith and a lot of hard work for me to go from the Marilyn of the past to who I am today. There is no magical formula that instantly erases the emotional effects of trauma in our lives. It is a life-long process, and it is a process that begins with and is continually directed by choices we make along the way.

When the heart has been damaged and needs healing, the choices that must be made are choices that must be made **intentionally**. You can either choose to take the path of least resistance or you can choose the path of healing and recovery. Working **hard** at this choice is not the key. However, working **smart** is the key to successful transformation!

The Right Tools

In order to work smart, you must have the right tools. The instrument that lights our path more than any other is God's Word. Combined with truth and obedience, it is the most powerful tool on earth.

Applied in the right way, God's word can shock you, humble you, and empower you to make long-term changes!

The path of least resistance is essentially staying where you are, not turning off the path that has been cleared for you by your past - the path prepared by your series of unfortunate events. Some refer to it as letting "Mother Nature" take her course. It's letting past generations effect the present generation. It's letting present decision-making, actions, character, and level of integrity be dictated by what you came from, the path you've been on thus far, and the factors that you may or may not have had any control over.

I have found that we as adults may choose not to follow the advice of our parents, but following the path of our parent's character is as likely as the law of gravity taking place! In my opinion, there is only one way not to follow in the footsteps of our parents, and that is through God's consistent and divine power at work in our lives. All the self-control in the world was not enough for me not to follow in the path of my adoptive parents. They were the parents that were most present in my life and so their example was the most influential. When our parents example is not worth following, then we must have new impressions take the place of their example.

In order to break free from my history, I had to repeatedly make the decision to choose the path of healing and recovery. I made numerous choices that contradicted what my emotions told me to do. Although everyone's journey to emotional health is different, there are several tools that can be used to assist everyone.

As you read through the remainder of this book, be aware that if you can relate to any of the circumstances I found myself in, then you must be prepared. If you take the challenge to embrace your divinely appointed legacy, you **will** encounter resistance! Resistance comes in many forms, like confusion or chaotic thoughts. However, your safety depends on your ability to center your focus on the one true Author of peace and love.

Breaking Free from Chains that Bind

You may experience emotions that force you to face your broken heart. You may be required to face fears that are at times disabling. Perhaps you will be forced to face the fact that your heart has turned into a cold heart of stone. Be assured that many others as well as myself have encountered all of these and lived to see them victoriously overcome by the power that God offers each of us. **We can break the chains that our past has bound us with**. To break the chains of the past, we must embrace and submit to the highest power known to man - God's Word!

"Through our knowledge of Him who called us by His own goodness and glory, God's divine power has given us all we need for life and godliness. He gave us His great and precious promises so that we can participate in His divine nature and escape the corruption of the world which is caused by evil desires." (2 Peter 1:3-4). Those of us who have experienced abandonment must confess our resentment. We may feel resentment, jealousy, or envy when we see others who have relationships we do not have - relationships that bring affirmation, support, encouragement, or perhaps a sense of belonging that comes with family.

Thankful for Wounds

We **can** be thankful that we have experienced abandonment, thankful that we are a misfit, and thankful that we are different from those around us. It is because of our differences that we are able to have compassion for others. We can be especially thankful because our Lord and Maker delights in us. He quiets our soul with His love and He rejoices over us. (Zephaniah 3:17). It is to God that we can lift up our souls. It is in **Him** that we trust and will not be put to shame, because no one whose hope is in God is **ever** put to shame (Psalm 25:1-3a). We can approach His throne with confidence when we are at the end of ourselves. We can approach His throne with confidence knowing that He loves us. We can approach His throne with confidence knowing that He will never abandon the works of His hands for we **are** the very work of His hands. (Psalm 138:8). He brings us out of captivity so that we may bring Him joy, praise, and honor (Jeremiah 33:7).

Thank Him for the pain and bring Him joy as your faith is put into action! **Display His power as you act upon His truth!** Place your complete trust in His words. As you do, pray that your eyes will see you as **He** sees you! Pray that your ears will hear what **He** wants you to hear. Pray that the wounds within your heart and soul will be healed because of the power of **His** words! If you do this, you will turn from your painful ways and you will be healed! Then, your **Legacy** will be of Divine Appointment!

Chapter 4

Your Journey of Transformation

As you proceed on your journey of transformation, you must insure that you first build a strong foundation. At our core we all have some basic beliefs about ourselves.

Those who were loved and cherished appropriately throughout their childhood have an instinctive knowledge of who they are. They internally have had the basic foundational needs met for security, significance, and stability. They know that they are going to be okay and feel **secure** because they always have been secure regardless of what is occurring around them. They know that they are **significant** and valued by those in their family. They know they are **stable** and whatever circumstances come their way, they will likely be equipped to handle it.

The Fatherless

If you did not have these foundational needs met, then you need to begin rebuilding the internal foundational beliefs of who you are.

I have found as a Marriage and Family Therapist for 30 years now, that the most effective method for rebuilding our core beliefs is to re-parent ourselves using the ultimate truth to override the non-truths. This process must begin with your belief about what makes you secure, significant, and stable!

I am made by Him and formed by Him so He is my creator and my Father (Deuteronomy 32:6b). Though I was fatherless, I can have security, significance, and stability at my core because of His parenting of my soul!

I am secure because my Creator carries me on His shoulders and has kept me the apple of His eye (Luke 15:5 and Deuteronomy 32:10-12). I have an anchor of hope which makes my soul firm and secure (Hebrews 6:19) regardless of my circumstances.

I am significant because my Creator has engraved me upon the palms of His hands (Isaiah 49:16). I am valued by Him as He delights and rejoices over me (Zephaniah 3:17).

I am stable because my Creator is my strength as He is the one who carries me, sustains me, and rescues me (Isaiah 46:3¬4). I have internal tenacity as a result of Him always being with me, never leaving me, or abandoning the works of His hands (Deuteronomy 31:6 & Psalm 138:8).

The Surrender

Consistency is required to counter my negative feelings with God's truth. Only then will my mind and my heart be transformed. Romans 12:1-2 talks about being transformed by the renewing of your mind. Renewing your mind can happen through the process of journaling or having a daily time with God where you take the lies you've been programmed to believe and surrender them to what God says. In our surrender to Him we will be **transformed!**

As you move forward on your journey pray that your Father will allow His divine power to enable you to live life with an awareness of what He perceives in you and what He created you for. His power will push out the lies that you have believed about yourself, if you are willing to do your part. Allow Him to re-parent you with His truths! Know that you are secure, significant and stable because of God!

My prayer for you is that your heart will receive God's truth in the pages that follow. Some of the New International Version scripture has been adjusted slightly to reflect instruction and guidance. I encourage you to pray, get out your Bible, journal as you read, and allow His truth to permeate every facet of your thoughts. Remember, **He** is your hiding place. **He** will protect you and give you songs of deliverance (Psalm 32:7)!

With great anticipation for all
God will do to heal your legacy,
Diane

God's Love Letter to Me

Dear (insert your name here),

Since you are precious and honored in my sight and because I love you...do not be afraid for I am with you!

You are my servant, whom I have chosen so that you may know and believe and understand that I am God.

No one can deliver you out of my hand!

I provide water in the desert and streams in the wasteland so that my chosen people whom I formed for myself will proclaim my praise!

You are one of my chosen. I blot out your transgression for my own sake! I will go before you and give you treasures and riches that are stored in secret places so that you may know that I am the Lord who summons you by name!

My purpose will stand and I will do all that I please. I am He who sustains you. I made you, I will carry you, and I will rescue you!

Though others may intend to harm you, I will accomplish good from harmful intentions. I will see to it that it all works together for your good!

Though someone in your life may have forgotten you, I will not forget you! You are engraved on the palms of my Hands!

Your Maker,
God

Genesis 50:20

Isaiah 43: 4, 5, 10, 20, & 21

Isaiah 45: 2-4

Isaiah 46: 1-4

Isaiah 49:15-16

Romans 8:28

Chapter 5

Strategies for Using God's Word

Step 1 - Remodeling the Foundation:

Our life is a lot like a building. When a building has a strong, well-built foundation, changes can be made to the building without having to totally rebuild it. Floors can be added, updating can be done, the entire façade can be replaced. However, when the foundation is faulty, eventually the entire building will have to be rebuilt, including the foundation, if that building is going to stand the test of time.

When a child is given a strong foundation, one in which they are left with a healthy self-esteem, it is because they were raised with a sense of **security, significance,** and **stability.** These children will more than likely be able to successfully face whatever life brings. Having healthy self-esteem is like a building with a well-built foundation. Minor and major life changes can be made, relationships can be lost or added, losses can be faced, and repairs can be made more easily because of the foundation of a healthy self-esteem.

When a child is not raised with a strong foundation, their experiences in life become more difficult to navigate through. Their faulty self-esteem does not give them the tools to successfully deal with life. If they are to be successful, they will need to undertake the emotionally painful task of tearing out the faulty foundation and replacing it with a healthy one. One that includes a sense of security, a place of significance, and an environment of stability.

Each of us have a foundation, something we base our life on. This foundation can be one that is based on truth or it can be based on lies.

My first step toward rebuilding my foundation began when the girl at school shared with me how much Jesus loved me. When I made the decision to accept His love my life took a turn that was both hopeful and healthy. However, if I had stopped there I would not have gotten very far. I had to allow His love to change my life so I started the arduous task of removing the faulty foundation and building a healthy one.

The next phase is just as important and is a process that will last the rest of my life. I started building a relationship with Christ. I started reading the Bible and learning from there how much God loves me and how He wanted me to live my life. My purpose for living was being reshaped by what God said about me in His Word.

I als started praying. I talked to God about what was going on in my life, about how much it hurt, and about the changes I wanted to see in myself. I also started listening. I started getting quiet and still and listening for that subtle, small voice that God so often uses to speak to us.

However, the main thing I had to learn to do in this new relationship was to start to trust God. Trusting anyone was not something that came easily for me because of the abuse I had been through and learning to trust someone I couldn't see made it even more difficult. Yet I had to start somewhere.

Step 2 - Forming Trust:

While I was still living in the abusive circumstances, I had a little place that I looked at as my refuge, my safe place. It was in the front yard on a steep incline. The front yard sloped down slightly and then there was a sharp incline where a very large bush sat. In the middle of that bush, there was a hollow space. And nobody knew about that hollow space but me.

My heart began its transformation in that hollow. When I was abused and running away from my abusers, most of the time crying and desperate for safety, I would run out of the back door of the house, around the side, and across the front yard, sliding into the bushes and out of sight of everyone. As I would slide onto the incline and into the hollow of the bush, I knew that I would be safe. No one but God could see me in that hollow.

I remember spending a lot of time in that hollow talking to God. One day during the time when the abuse was at its worst, I was sitting on my feet with my knees pulled close to my face. I remember holding my knees and crying to God and saying, "If you're really real and you can really hear me, all I want to do is graduate high school. But I don't think I'm going to live that long." I begged God to do whatever it would take to help me to live long enough to graduate, then I would know I wasn't dumb. That was my big goal in life, to know I wasn't dumb.

This time when I prayed, I remember it felt different. When I was praying, I felt what I now know as God's presence. I felt a sense of peace. And I heard something. It wasn't audible, but I heard the words "you will and then some." I knew God was telling me, "You will graduate from high school, and then some."

As I look back on it now, I understand what He meant. At that time, though, I didn't care about "and then some." I just wanted to live long enough to graduate from high school! But those words began to prompt me to thank Him for letting me graduate, even though I did not see how it was possible.

I'm not alone in having had trauma in my life. We all have had trauma of some kind and to some extent. Perhaps your trauma wasn't to the severity of mine but because of your trauma you too need a safe place. You won't overcome your particular trauma without it. So where is your safe place? Who is your safe place? My first safe place was the hollow on that hill side, but then I was given other safe places like my third house which I finally got to call "home." We all need the safety of mentors like I had in Beth's father (my third dad) and my counselor Dan along with his wife, Jenna, and my father and mother-in-law who are still mentors to me today. We must be prudent in choosing people who are safe. Having mentors like I have had, has given me earthly examples of what it looks like to walk with integrity and moral character. These are just a few people in my life that have been guiding lights for me to admire and lean on when I cannot see my way.

Where do you turn when you're desperate, when you're at the end of what you can do for yourself? Create and discover your own safe place where you can be alone to be still and hear His voice, feel His presence and allow His peace to comfort you. The peace that you will feel in your own "hollow" will be of divine appointment so take the time to meet Him in that place.

Step 3 - Acting on Faith:

In that hollow where I was desperate and at the end of myself, was where I began my trust and dependence in God. The answers I received from Him went against logic. I could not envision living long enough to graduate high school but I cautiously started to believe Him.

Believing Him is why I got up that one Friday morning and walked out of the abusive house. It wasn't planned. It was a split second decision. I just knew. I didn't know why but I knew it was time to leave. I didn't know where I was going but I knew I had to get out.

I believe that split-second decision was the culmination of the previous year and the result of time spent focused on God's words to me, which was beginning to change my decision-making. It was the result of God helping me to focus and re-evaluate my life's purpose. It was God's way of saving my life and showing me the wonderful purpose for which He created me.

Running away from that house Friday morning was a **huge** step toward discovering my faith in God and His purpose for my life. But it was just one step of many I took down the path of healing and recovery. The most difficult step was getting out of my comfort zone and taking risks as I made awkward and clumsy attempts to face my failures and my inability to help myself. Believing what you cannot explain with logic requires faith. When I took that first step, my faith was so very small and I had many reasons to freeze up and not take action.

I have had many failures since that Spring morning in 1976. Each time I have faced a challenge, God has purged more of my faulty thinking, which is sometimes so embedded within my heart that I have to learn some lessons repeatedly. Even today when I am faced with a challenge, I am slow to remember that God wants to show me something about myself through my present circumstance.

When I am intentionally looking for what He has me to learn, I go back to looking at my foundation and evaluate where my trust lies. I ask myself from whom am I seeking my safety? My security? Who do I look to in order for peace? For stability? Who gives me my significance?

This requires my heart to go back to my "hollow" and be still before my maker and listen as my soul becomes quiet with rest. Psalm 51:6 tells us "Surely you desire truth in the inner parts, you teach me wisdom in the inmost place". I thank Him for revealing to me the truth about myself, purging me of faulty thinking, and teaching me wisdom within my heart. He began speaking to me in the "hollow" and I am forever grateful for my time there.

I sometimes ask God to test me and know my anxious thoughts and see if there is any offensive way within me and lead me in the way He wants me to go. (I got that idea from Psalm 139:23-24.) If you choose to use this particular tool, be prepared to see some ugly things about yourself which you alone are responsible for. That is what happens to me each and every time I go there with God. His blessings are always bigger than my unveiling.

If you trust Him enough to take action based on His Word and not allow your emotion to prompt your action, then you will be blessed beyond measure. Trust Him in your own hollow. Trust Him for your security and safety. Trust Him for your value and significance. Trust Him for your stability because His love is never going to leave you.

Chapter 6

Strategies for Repairing the Heart

One of the major things that must happen in order for us to continue our path of healing and recovery is we have to change our self-talk. Within our hearts we talk to ourselves. This is called self-talk and reveals what we believe about ourselves. For most of us, our self-talk reflects our parents' messages to us in childhood.

Step 1 - Identifying the Ugly Lies:

I grew up being told that I was ugly and dumb. Frequently, I was told that I couldn't do anything right and that nobody liked me and no one would ever love me. The common theme of the messages I received from my adoptive parents was that I was "too dumb to ever amount to anything." These messages were ugly lies. Parents often will use words they do not believe because they are in pain. Unresolved pain can cause us to say things we do not mean.

Because I was young and easily influenced, I believed every word they said about me. I didn't doubt anything they said, because I had no other opinion to counter theirs until I spent time in my Bible.

Those lies were part of the faulty foundation upon which my life was built. The foundation had to go and something had to replace it! The first chip torn out of that faulty foundation came on the day I believed in God and decided to accept His love for me. I was able to begin to believe that God thought I was worth more than what others thought I was worth. The first evidence of that change was when I believed I was worthy to sit in an actual seat on the school bus.

Step 2 - Replacing Lies with Truth:

Over time, more and more chips were removed from my faulty foundation. I began to replace the ugly lies that I had been told with truths. I read in the Bible how God felt about me. I heard sermons about God's love for me when I would sneak off to church with Ellen's family. I spent time with God in "The Hollow" and began to trust that He had a good plan for my life.

After I left the abusive house and began living in my new home, my new family told me that they loved me. I wasn't just told with their words but also by their actions. I experienced God's love lived out through a real family for the very first time. Consequently, more and more of those ugly lies were removed from my faulty foundation.

However, there was still a lot of work left to do. The steps I had taken were **huge.** And I was no longer living in the environment where I physically heard the lies about me. But all of that did not erase the recordings of those lies that continued to play in my head. I didn't learn how to combat those lies until I was in college.

Step 3 - Journaling Emotions:

During my freshman year of college, I received a letter from my abusive mother. The letter informed me that her husband had died six months earlier of Lou Gehrig's disease (ALS). It had been a very painful process. She went on to explain that he died because of me leaving them with all the work to be done with the animals which in turn caused his premature death.

Self-Looking

The letter was threatening, angry and hostile. Unfortunately, I took it to heart and believed the accusations of it being my fault that my adoptive father had died. This caused a plethora of chaotic thoughts, false guilt that disabled me, and a slow build of uncontrollable rage. I was in an emotional crisis and it was this crisis that led me to my first professional counseling appointment.

I believed what the letter said about me because I still had old parenting messages in my head. "I was created to work and work is the only things I'm good for." I was in a state of confusion and struggled with the fact that I had run away from them in order to protect myself.

My geography had changed and I changed my name but my self-image, my self-talk, and my foundational belief about myself had not changed. I still believed about myself the same lies I had been told while growing up. Fortunately, my counselor was a kind and wise man who saw potential in me.

Counseling

My first counselor, Dan, was big on me working hard to change, taking responsibility for my current feelings, and on homework. I thought to myself at the time, "Well isn't that what he was there for? Wasn't it his job to do the work? I was here and willing to talk, he should do the hard stuff. After all, I'm the one who survived the whole ordeal!" I felt that the human race, the world, or maybe God owed me, and everyone should just cut me a little slack!

The first homework assignment Dan gave me was for me to write a letter to my abusive mother. In this letter, I was to say exactly how I felt. It didn't have to be logical. It didn't have to make sense. It just had to be honest. It had to say exactly how offended and hurt I felt by what she had done to me and said about me.

Dan told me that the beauty of this kind of unfiltered letter is in the fact that it would never be sent! I could be completely honest with her concerning my real feelings with no fear of retribution.

This was the first type of journaling that I learned...the unfiltered letter. And I have used it many times since then. It is a very safe method of expressing honest feelings without fear of retaliation. It is amazing the effect that writing such a letter has on one who has been unjustly treated.

The unfiltered truth about how I felt at that time was filled with ugly feelings that had been sitting inside for years just festering and boiling and bubbling with resentment and hostility. When the truth comes out it is often quite ugly to look at. But just like an infection that has set in on our physical body, it may smell and look distasteful and ugly, but revealing it is the only way to be cleansed of it.

Still more amazing is the effect it has when the one who has been wronged is reading the letter out loud! You see, Dan had failed to inform me that in my next session I was going to have to read the letter out loud for him to hear! Sort of sneaky, if you ask me, but very effective at getting the truth out and beginning the healing process!

UgLies

I believe journaling can be used as a purging process. Honest journaling reveals my "ugLIES". Once those are revealed, I can compare them to God's truth. Then choosing to believe God's truth over my "ugLIES" purges out whatever is standing in the way of me being everything God created me to be. That is the beginning of the process. Key word being **process**. There is no magical formula. It is something I will do for the rest of my life but it is also worth every minute of it!

We all have self-talk, whether we realize it or not. And our self-talk can be either good or bad. It's good if it's helping you fulfill God's purpose for your life. For some people good self-talk may be self-talk that's helping you heal and recover from your past. Most of us experience at least some bad or negative self-talk on a regular basis.

Journaling is a major tool I've used over the years to change my self-talk. The point of journaling is to change the way I think. I call journaling "Gettin' Out the UgLIES and Puttin' in the Truth". I consider the "ugLIES" to be lies that I believe about myself or about life that are hindering me from being the person God created me to be. The "ugLIES" would consist of anything to do with fear, anxiety, shame, anger, lack of self-worth, neediness, intolerance of others, judgments of others, greed, envy, anything contrary to God's best and His purpose for me and anything that makes me feel unlovable.

Honest Journaling

In order for any type of journaling to be therapeutic, it has to be honest. It has to be real. It has to be unfiltered. I believe they are personal and are to be kept private. There may be rare occasions when you share an excerpt with your therapist or possibly with your spouse. But for the most part, the only person who should know what you've written in your journal other than you is God. He can handle the blunt honesty no matter how ugly it may be. In fact, He already knows how you're feeling and what you're thinking even before you figure it out.

There are different ways to journal. One way I've already mentioned is writing unfiltered letters. Other forms of journaling that I've used are journaling emotions, dreams, and guilt. However, journaling is not repeating yourself over and over on paper. This would not be healthy.

Here's an example of how I journal emotions. If I am having a day filled with feelings of being ugly or stupid. My first counselor, Dan, taught me to go deeper and determine **why** I was feeling ugly or stupid. So I get out my notebook and start writing down exactly how I feel. My journal entry may look like this:

Today I feel ugly because:

I've gained a couple of pounds

I have a pimple

I'm having a bad hair day

Or maybe:

Today I feel stupid because:

I spilled my tea

I dropped my book

I told a joke and no one laughed but me

I shared what I thought was a great idea and others did not

agree with me

Then I find in the Bible, or write down from memory, scriptures or truths about God's view of me. Then I write down the discrepancies between the lie and the truth.

I feel ugly, but does that mean I am ugly? How can I really be ugly when God tells me that "I am fearfully and wonderfully made" (Psalm 139:14) and that "He dances over me with joy", and that I am the "crown of His creation"?

Or how can I be stupid when I am "made in His image", "created in His likeness", and "I am the work of His Hands and He will not abandon me"(Psalm 138:8b)?

So I write down my feelings and then counter them with truths from God's word. I also recognize that I am human, and because I'm human, I'm going to have bad hair days. But I counter the feelings of ugliness and stupidity with facts about who God says I am.

A Changed Mind

Romans 12:1-2 talks about being transformed by the renewing of your mind. That's self-talk! Renewing your mind can happen through the process of journaling, or having a daily time with God where you take the "ugLIES" and compare them to what He says and get rid of the "ugLIES" and make a decision to believe the truths. That's where **transformation** begins!

Stupid In = Stupid Out

If I continue to be pre-occupied with negative feelings and focus on them, then I will stay "tied up" on the inside. What happens next is, I lose the real me, that I was created to be, all as a result of me acting out the feelings that I am focused on. Some refer to this as self-fulfilling prophecy. I agree but it is also a version of "as a man thinks in his heart so is he" or "out of the overflow of the heart the mouth speaks"

(Matthew 12:34). If I believe in my heart that I am stupid, I act stupid and others pick up on how I think of myself and they begin to treat me as if I am stupid. The vicious cycle begins.

Next I pray...Father, Your divine power enables me to live life with an awareness of what I was created for. Your power pushes out the lies that I have believed about myself whether those lies came from me or other people. But in order to live this out, I must participate with you and your divine calling on my life.

Then I spend some time in God's word looking for truths about how God sees me. Making a list of what I believe God created me to be as opposed to what I was feeling. So even though I might be feeling like the list I originally wrote down, I choose to believe (and I write down) what God created me to be.

Example:

> God created me to be:
>
> Spunky, kind to animals, in control of myself, energetic, one who loves to take walks, confident in God, a thinker, someone who is determined and tenacious in looking for the positive and the potential in situations, and one who is creative in looking for the good in impossible situations.

Some days I may write down that I'm feeling:

> Needy, unsteady, old, overly sensitive, unlovable, fat or ugly.

And then I'll counter that with scripture like the following:

> You made my inner being the way it is.
> I am fearfully and wonderfully made. (Psalm 139:13-14)
>
> I am your clay, you are my potter,
> I am the work of your Hand. (Isaiah 64:8)

You have given me a crown of beauty instead of ashes,
gladness instead of mourning,
and a spirit of praise instead of despair. (Isaiah 61:3)

All my days are in your book
before one of them came to be (Psalm 139:16)

I am always with you (Psalm 139:18b)

You set me free from my own prison.
you do that so I can praise You. (Psalm 142:7)

Truth In = Truth Out

These are truths and they will set us free of our "ugLIES". So every time I get the "ugLIES", I write down my feelings and then counter them with scripture. As those uninvited feeling come up during the day, I replace them with scripture. It doesn't have to be a whole verse, just a little portion that relates to that feeling.

For me, my poor self-esteem was a result of my value being based on lies and on other people's opinions instead of God's opinions. That resulted in me having pop-up thoughts like, "I'm so stupid, I'm so dumb" as well as other lies and negative opinions that I was taught.

For you, it may be different lies. God wants to put truth in the place of those lies. But we have to do our part which is to recognize the lies and search out truth that counters the lies. When the pop¬up thoughts come, we must consciously replace them with the truth. It takes discipline and is essential in order to restructure thoughts based on truth instead of being based on how I feel.

Step 4 - Journaling Dreams:

Journaling is also very useful when dealing with traumatic dreams or dreams that have pieces of your unpleasant past in them. Dreams are typically a release of bits and pieces of the subconscious. When reviewing your dream, you need to focus on the dominant emotions in the dream. Is it fear, anxiety, shame, anger, or trying to get control of something that's out of your control? What is the emotion that is driving your dream?

When I begin to dream things that cause me to wake up in a cold sweat, or I have a nightmare, or the dream itself is traumatic, a healthy first step is writing out the dream as soon as I wake up because the longer we're awake, the more aspects of the dream we will forget.

Re-Shaping

The next step is to put myself in the position of acting as a playwright, or the producer of a play. I change the ending of the dream on paper. This process is called **reshaping a dream.**

When writing the new ending, I incorporate the truths that I know reflect God's view of me and His view of justice. The same truths I use to counter my feelings when journaling my emotions. I then put myself in a place in the dream where I have control over the things God intended for me to have control over.

For example, I have a right over my body, who touches it, and in what way. Those boundaries are mine to control. So if I'm having a traumatic dream where those boundaries are being crossed, I rewrite the dream so that in the dream I reinforce the boundary, stand up for myself in a confident manner, and the other person listens. If I do that frequently enough, then my dreams actually start to change.

The way I look at it is if we put the truth into our head repeatedly, it becomes an instinctive response that even permeates our dreams. Working on positive self-talk in our waking hours eventually helps us manage the anxiety that pops up in our dreams. By doing this little exercise we have re-instated a small amount of volitional control in our lives and the need for transformation continues.

Step 5 - Journaling Shame and Guilt:

Another issue some adults deal with who had a less than perfect childhood is distinguishing between real guilt and false guilt. Based on what we were raised to believe is right and wrong, some of us enter adulthood with an overly sensitive conscience. In other words, the faulty foundation we are handed by our parents may leave us feeling guilty about some things we do or say or feel, when in reality before our Creator we are not wrong.

Identify the Source

Dealing with false guilt can also be dealt with by writing down exactly what we're feeling guilty about in bullet points and then find truths from God's word that help us determine whether or not this is real guilt or false guilt.

Here are a few ways I use to tell the difference: God's conviction is Christ-centered; false guilt is self-centered. God's conviction brings hope for change; false guilt causes us to be paralyzed in hopelessness. God's conviction brings grace; false guilt brings condemnation. Condemnation is based on lies sometimes with elements of truth interwoven. The one who condemns us is our enemy, the devil. He is the master of accusations. So, if we listen, we will be living a condemned life.

Boldly Making Amends

"For the sake of your name, Lord, forgive my iniquity, though it is great." (Psalm 25:11) I believe real guilt, conviction, comes from God and helps us see what we have done wrong and gives us hope. We make amends when we confess and for the sake of His name in our lives He will forgive us because we have humbled ourselves. If we find that we are dealing with false guilt or shame, we will need to continue journaling and continue replacing the lies we were taught with the truths we find in God's word.

As we continue on our path of healing and recovery we must remember to be bold and stouthearted. We must not waiver in our confusion because the one thing that is worthy of all of our trust and all of our dependence is God's love for us. It is the only love that is 100% reliable. "The eyes of the Lord are on those who fear him, on those whose hope is in his unfailing love…We wait in hope for the Lord, he is our help and our shield." (Psalm 33:18-20).

Here are some additional scriptures that helped me while I journaled.

Psalm 31
1 O Lord, I have come to you for protection;
don't let me be disgraced.
Save me, for you do what is right.
2 Turn your ear to listen to me;
rescue me quickly.
Be my rock of protection,
a fortress where I will be safe.
3 You are my rock and my fortress.
For the honor of your name, lead me out of this danger.
4 Pull me from the trap that my enemies set for me,

for I find protection in you alone.
5 I entrust my spirit into your hand.
Rescue me, Lord, for you are a faithful God.

Psalm 139: 1-18 and 23-24

1 O LORD, you have searched me
and you know me.
2 You know when I sit and when I rise;
you perceive my thoughts from afar.
3 You discern my going out and my lying down;
you are familiar with all my ways.
4 Before a word is on my tongue
you know it completely, O LORD.
5 You hem me in—behind and before;
you have laid your hand upon me.
6 Such knowledge is too wonderful for me,
too lofty for me to attain.
7 Where can I go from your Spirit?
Where can I flee from your presence?
8 If I go up to the heavens, you are there;
if I make my bed in the depths, you are there.
9 If I rise on the wings of the dawn,
if I settle on the far side of the sea,
10 even there your hand will guide me,
your right hand will hold me fast.
11 If I say, "Surely the darkness will hide me
and the light become night around me,"
12 even the darkness will not be dark to you;
the night will shine like the day,
for darkness is as light to you.
13 For you created my inmost being;

you knit me together in my mother's womb.
14 I praise you because I am fearfully and wonderfully made;
your works are wonderful,
I know that full well.
15 My frame was not hidden from you
when I was made in the secret place.
when I was woven together in the depths of the earth,
16 your eyes saw my unformed body.
All the days ordained for me
were written in your book
before one of them came to be.
17 How precious to me are your thoughts,[a] God!
How vast is the sum of them!
18 Were I to count them,
they would outnumber the grains of sand—
when I awake, I am still with you.
23 Search me, O God, and know my heart;
test me and know my anxious thoughts.
24 See if there is any offensive way in me,
and lead me in the way everlasting.

You are on your way to **Strategically Repairing your Heart.** As you do, remember these steps:

1. Make a list of your "UgLies."
2. Make a list of God's truth about you.
3. Journal emotion.
4. Journal dreams.
5. Journal the guilt and shame.

Chapter 7

Strategies for Healing the Hurt

Max Lucado points out in his book Facing Your Giants, we must face our pain with tears, time and truth . . . like David did when he embraced his grief over the loss of his friend, Jonathan. David writes in the Psalms of "flushing the hurt out of our hearts." I don't know how deep the pain goes within your heart but I do know that however deep the pain goes, you must flush the hurt out of your heart to the same extent. Some people will not understand this. In fact, well-meaning people, even religious or spiritual leaders, will encourage you to get over it and move on, to put the past in the past. In an effort to follow this well meaning and misguided advice, we repress the hurt, push forward, and end up carrying a heavy burden.

Step 1 - Taking Time to Feel the Hurt:

Take it from someone who knows all too well the depth of pain that can be within your soul, **you must take time to hurt if you are**

ever going to heal! Resolving the pain and healing the hurt will take time. Not just a little time, especially if the infliction of the pain and the resulting consequences were spread over a long period of time. However, it doesn't mean that it must take a lifetime of grieving to overcome your pain.

There are many ways that people are hurt in life. You possibly lost a parent to death. Or maybe you lost them because they made poor choices. You need to take time to grieve the loss of your parent(s). Maybe you lost your innocence before you were old enough to know how to spell the word, much less to comprehend its meaning. You must take time to embrace that loss and grieve your lost childhood. Take time to grieve by allowing yourself to feel your loss and express it in a physical manner. For some, that is with tears and for others it is best expressed through writing.

Hurting People Hurt People

Whatever its source, you must face your pain with truth and with the courage to do whatever it takes for however long it takes to flush it all out of your heart and soul. And when it returns, flush it out again. You must stop trying to ignore it and you must take the time to face it. Remember, when people have unresolved hurt hidden deep within their hearts, they will in turn hurt others.

Step 2 - Facing the Truth about Yourself:

During my first year of college people would ask me where I was from. I remember making the decision the first day of freshman orientation that I would pretend I came from a normal family. So when someone would ask me a question about my family, I would tell them about my new loving parents, my sisters, and how wonderful they were. When they asked me why my last name wasn't the same, I would quickly distract them by changing the subject.

I tried to hide from the truth. I tried to hide my past. I didn't want to face it or talk about it. But the more deceiving I did and the more I repressed my feelings, the more hurt and angry I became. And then I got the letter telling me about my adoptive father's death which led me into counseling.

Facing the Hurt

My counselor told me **not** to hide the truth about my past. Instead he said I should **embrace** it. He told me I had to face the truth about my past and the resulting consequences. He explained that I had to take an honest look at the differences between me and my peers—like the fact that I didn't have a mother like the other girls in my dorm, and that I never would, but that I could still be okay. He explained that as I faced the differences, I needed to grieve them.

Facing the hurt and the anger is not easy or quick. Again, it is a process that takes time. The alternative to this process is living life hiding from the truth. Hiding from the truth is like taking pain killers to take away the pain from a bad tooth. I can keep medicating or I can go see a dentist and actually take care of the problem. So to face the pain, you must embrace it, you must engage in the pain. **Don't just report the hurt, express the hurt!** That is the only way you can move beyond it.

Years ago, little boys used to play with marbles. Some of them would stuff their pockets so full of marbles that eventually a pocket seam would rip. Then everywhere they went, you could tell where they had been, because you could follow the trail of marbles that had fallen out of their pocket.

When we have unresolved hurt, we leave a trail of raw feelings everywhere we go. We stuff it and stuff it and say, "Oh, I'm okay, it doesn't bother me". We may find ourselves saying "There are a lot of people who have endured a lot more than I have." Or, "I don't want to think about that right now." Or "I'm just going to try and forget that happened and hopefully these ugly feelings will go away."

When we do this, we are stuffing our emotions. Eventually the seams of our life rip open and everywhere we go, we leave a trail. A trail of people that **we've** now hurt. Remember, people with unresolved hurts hurt other people. The only way to resolve the hurt is to turn and face the truth about our pain and embrace it, express it, and deal with it.

Step 3 - Getting Angry in a Healthy Way:

Hurt and anger are like strange bedfellows. In an effort to ignore our hurt, we repress our hurt instead of dealing with it. Eventually that repressed hurt turns into repressed anger. A good way to see if you have hurt that you need to deal with is to evaluate how you react to current situations that may elicit similar emotion. If something happens that makes you angry, evaluate your anger on a scale of one to ten. Then take where your anger is on the scale and compare it to what level of anger is warranted in this situation without an effect from the history. How would others who are healthy and balanced in their anger react in this situation?

Home Grown Anger

If you are like me at all, you may find yourself in a situation where you have deeply rooted home-grown anger. My anger was embedded deep within my heart. I know this because I was consistently angrier than what was reasonable. If you find yourself consistently angrier than you think is reasonable, there's an excellent chance you have some unresolved hurt and anger you need to deal with. If others tell you that you over-react in your anger or react too quickly, chances are very good that your reaction to the current situation is being affected by old anger and that there's a common denominator between this situation and an old one that you have yet to resolve.

When we attempt to develop discernment in these situations, we must keep in mind what God's view of anger is. I read in Psalm 4:4 that when we are angry we should not sin, but instead we should search our hearts and be quiet. To do this we are in need of complete honesty. For example, we are justified to be disappointed when traffic prevents us from accomplishing our goals on time. However, is my level of anger warranted? If your answer is "yes, because people drive like idiots!" then I challenge you to re-examine (search your heart) what is driving the anger.

A person who has been hurt and who has not dealt with the hurt is easily offended, easily angered, and easily hurt. They have a heart with old hurt in it. When people act unreasonable and obnoxious, there's a reason. People don't just wake up one day and say, "I'm going to be difficult and angry for the rest of my life." It comes from hurts that have built up over the years and have not been dealt with.

On the other side of the coin, we should not allow hurt people to mistreat us, but we should have compassion for them. This compassion might make us think before just reacting to them. Think and consider what hurt might be playing havoc within them and robbing them of their joy. Be mindful of responding in a way that is protective of yourself and yet respectful of them.

Old Anger = Fear

Repressed anger can also lead to developing a defensive posture with unreasonable expectations. If we haven't dealt with our anger, we may think, "Oh, look what happened to me, I'm a victim and therefore I deserve special treatment." Then when your expectations for this special treatment are disappointed, you end up being angry again which leads us to feel more shame, more hurt, and even fear.

The fear comes from feeling like you have no control over certain aspects of your life. And once you begin to fear, your fear can cause you to try to control or maneuver everybody around you and become manipulative. That creates unhealthy relationships and perpetuates a vicious cycle of repressed anger, exaggerated expectations, perceived control over others, disappointed expectations, and more hurt and anger that's not dealt with.

Step 4 - Embracing Emotion to Avoid Desperation:

There's a desperation that comes to people who have a lot of hurt built up. They have a **sense of urgency** to have things go the way they expect them to go, the way that in their minds they think things should go. Hurt people prefer to maintain control because they are afraid to not be in control. The attempts to be in control are not necessarily bad for others, just frustrating. Life is often unpredictable and requires flexibility.

Time Bombs

Most of us with built up hurt aren't just disappointed when things do not occur as expected. Instead of just being slightly irritated or bothered, our old wounds begin to **hurt.** If you have been traumatized or hurt in the past you may try to move beyond it by trying not to think about it. But the trauma and hurt is still sitting there and we can become walking time bombs.

If we never take the time to deal with the hurt and the anger, we will eventually explode or implode. Some will explode, which will be immediately obvious to whoever is around them. Some will implode. This inward explosion can be in the form of depression or anxiety attacks or it can take some physical form like self-mutilation.

We must give ourselves permission to feel the anger. Only by feeling the anger can we truly process it and get beyond it. Even Jesus was angry. We can see one incident where he was angry by reading Mark 3:1-5. He became angry and deeply distressed at the Pharisees and their stubborn hearts as they reacted to Him healing a cripple on the Sabbath. If Jesus got angry, then who are we to avoid our anger?

Step 5 - Be Brave Enough to Face Discomfort:

When we're hurting and angry, whether it's a current or an unresolved issue from our past, we have a choice to make. We can choose to take time out from what we're doing and turn and face the pain head-on, or we can ignore it. We can push it aside, distract ourselves with busyness, eat, take a nap, go on a shopping trip, or watch a television show. We all have many ways we distract ourselves. This is the easy way and the path of least resistance. It requires no bravery. It only requires a desire to be comfortable.

The Influence of Hurt

"If we call on Him and he answers us, He will make us **bold** and stouthearted." (Psalm 138:3). If we want to be brave and **stouthearted,** we must look at what makes us hurt. The past will influences us. You cannot get away from that. The question is **how** is it going to influence you? If you turn around and look at the pain from your past and embrace it, God can use it for good in your life! As opposed to it being a weight that keeps dragging you down through the rest of your life.

Dealing with the pain from your past and the resulting hurt and anger takes time and honesty. Honesty is what prompts you to take a deep look inward at the pain and to **take responsibility for the status of the pain.** It's a willingness to be completely honest that I am today being affected by my past in a negative way.

Once we make the decision to process the hurt, we then have another choice to make. We can now either continue to focus on the cruelty of the offender or we can turn and focus on the kindness and compassion of God.

Choosing Boldness that Leads to Peace

So whether we're writing in a journal, or yelling aloud to God, or crying and venting to a counselor, we must choose to express the hurt. We will be more at peace if we choose to end that time with refocusing ourselves on the compassion and the kindness that we have in our relationship with God.

This isn't a one-time action. It is a choice we must make every time we're hurt, whether from the past or the present. If we continue to choose to focus on the cruelty of the offense, we will continue to feel like a powerless victim and we will stay stuck in our pain and with our anger. But if we choose to focus on God's love and compassion for us, we will continue to replace the pain with love and we will be able to become the person God created us to be. We can move from a place of being deeply wounded to a place of being grateful for the comfort we learn to receive from God. **It is your choice!**

Step 6 - Feeling the Comfort of God's Presence:

When we're hurting, I think we need to constantly remind our-selves of how much God loves us, how passionate He is about bring-ing healing to us, and how much He wants to help us in our healing and recovery process. God desires to intervene in our pain . . . but that doesn't always mean He's going to take away the pain. Many times that means He brings us comfort in the pain. One of the biggest ways he comforts us is with **His presence.** "God is always with you and He will quiet you with His love." (Zephaniah 3:17)

Recognize the Need

God is a personal God who loves us, heals us, helps us, and inter-venes in our pain. He does not wait for us to do the right thing be-fore He acts. I believe He looks for a God-hungry heart...a heart that recognizes its need for His presence. When we're hurting is when we need His presence the most.

Psalm 30:7: "LORD, when you favored me, you made my royal mountain stand firm; but when you hid your face, I was dismayed."

You are now on your way to strategically healing your wounds and becoming Forever Grateful! Remember to repeat these steps as often as needed:

1. Take Time to Hurt
2. Face the Truth about Yourself
3. Get Angry in a Healthy Way
4. Embrace Emotion to Avoid Desperation
5. Be Brave Enough to Face Discomfort
6. Feel the Comfort of God's Presence

My Love Letter to God

Dear God,

Thank you for choosing me to display your splendor. I am thankful that you called me by name to be your servant. (It is an honor and a privilege to serve you.)

Thank you for having compassion on me and for keeping me and for guiding me. I am grateful for you putting your words within my heart and showing me what is right.

Thank you for strengthening me and enabling me to not fear the reproach of people or to be terrified by their insults. Thank you for enabling me to stand for the afflicted and the helpless.

I praise you for healing me by your wounds and taking my sins on yourself. I am indebted to you forever because you have carried my sorrows. I am in awe of your love for me and your everlasting kindness!

I know that you revive the spirit of the lowly and heart of the contrite. You have guided me and satisfied my needs. You strengthen my frame and I am forever grateful for this! Help me to not go my own way or speak idle words but enable me to honor you with my words. Help me to call on you for justice and to plead with integrity. You have put your words in my mouth and placed your spirit in me and I am so thankful for this.

I praise you for planting me and allowing me to be the works of your hands. You planted me to be a display of your splendor and I am grateful. You are my potter, I am your clay! Because of this, help me to choose what pleases you and to always listen to you and avoid what is evil.

I am glad and I celebrate what you created! You created me to be your delight and to bring you joy. For a long time, I will enjoy the works of my hands because I was chosen by you! I hear your words and I am grate-

ful that you will repay your enemies all that they deserve and that you comfort me as a mother comforts her child. Your hand is made known to those who serve you and your fury to those who are your foes!

My heart rejoices that you will always look upon me as your people and that your hand is made known to all your servants. You have extended peace to me like a river and I glorify you. I praise you because you have loved me and I tremble at your words.

Your Creation,

(insert your name here)

Isaiah 49: 3, 5, 8, 10, 14   Isaiah 59: 4, 21
Isaiah 51: 7, 9, 12   Isaiah 60: 21-22
Isaiah 53: 5, 4, 8   Isaiah 64: 4 Isaiah 65:18
Isaiah 58: 12   Isaiah 66: 2, 5, 6, 12-14

Biblical Strategies for Healing My Legacy

I Redefined Myself by Using God's Words...
Breaking a Legacy of Destruction
and Embracing a Legacy of Hope!

Bold words denote author's paraphrase

My Significance...

I am the Apple of His eye...

For you created my inmost being; you knit me together in my mother's womb. I praise you because I am fearfully and wonderfully made; your works are wonderful, I know that full well.
Psalm 139:13-14

Since I am precious and honored in his sight, and because he loves me, he will give people in exchange for me, nations in exchange for my life.
Isaiah 43:4

Yet you, LORD, are my Father. I am the clay, you are the potter; I am the work of your hand.
Isaiah 64:8

Though my father and mother forsake me, the Lord will receive me.
Psalm 27:10

I call on you, my God, for you will answer me; turn your ear to me and hear my prayer. Keep me as the apple of your eye, hide me in the shadow of your wings.
Psalm 17:6, 8

The LORD your God is with me, the Mighty Warrior who saves. He will take great delight in me; in his love he will no longer rebuke me, but will rejoice over me with singing.
Zephaniah 3:17

My Security...

See, I have engraved you on the palms of my hands; your walls are ever before me.
Isaiah 49:16

The LORD will vindicate me; your love, Lord, endures forever— do not abandon the works of your hands.
Psalm 138:8

For you have been my hope, Sovereign Lord, my confidence since my youth. From birth I have relied on you; you brought me forth from my mother's womb. I will ever praise you.
Psalm 71:5-6

The Lord is the stronghold of my life - of whom shall I be afraid?
Psalm 27:1b

Then Jesus told them this parable: "Suppose one of you has a hundred sheep and loses one of them. Doesn't he leave the ninety-nine in the open country and go after the lost sheep until he finds it? And when he finds it, he joyfully puts it on his shoulders and goes home. Then he calls his friends and neighbors together and says, 'Rejoice with me; I have found my lost sheep.'
Luke 15:3-6

*I have this hope as an anchor for **my** soul, firm and secure.*
Hebrews 6:19a

My Stability...

The Sovereign Lord is my strength; he makes my feet like the feet of a deer, he enables me to tread on the heights.
Habakkuk 3:19

*He has upheld **me** since **my** birth, and has carried **me** since **I** was born. Even to **my** old age and gray hairs...**He** will sustain **me**. **He** has made **me** and **He** will carry **me**; **He** will sustain **me** and **He** will rescue **me**.*
Isaiah 46:3-4

I keep my eyes always on the LORD. With him at my right hand, I will not be shaken.
Psalm 16:8

The Lord is the stronghold of my life - of whom shall I be afraid? Though an army besiege me, my heart will not fear; though war break out against me, even then I will be confident. Though my father and mother forsake me, the Lord will receive me. Teach me your way, Lord; lead me in a straight path because of my oppressors.
Psalm 27: 1b, 3, 10-11

Guard my life and rescue me; do not let me be put to shame, for I take refuge in you. May integrity and uprightness protect me, because my hope, Lord, is in you.
Psalm 25:20-21

*Though **I** may stumble, **I** will not fall, for the Lord upholds **me** with his hand.*
Psalm 37:24

After re-structuring my foundation, I have used the following words as a peaceful guide for my daily life. In these words we can all find that God is...

A Comforter for those in pain

A Lover of the misfits

A Friend to the friendless

A Hope for the hopeless

A Father to the Fatherless!

My Abandonment...

Therefore my heart is glad and my tongue rejoices; my body also will rest secure, because you will not abandon me to the realm of the dead, nor will you let your faithful one see decay.
Psalm 16:9-10

Have I not commanded you? Be strong and courageous. Do not be afraid; do not be discouraged, for the Lord your God will be with you wherever you go.
Joshua 1:9

He took me from the ends of the earth, from its farthest corners He called me. He said, "I am his servant"; He has chosen me and has not rejected me. So do not fear, for He is with me; do not be dismayed, for He is my God. He will strengthen me and help me; He will uphold me with His righteous right hand.
Isaiah 41:9-10

My Angels...

*Angels are ministering spirits sent to serve **me** when I inherit salvation.*
Hebrews 1:14

*For He will command his angels concerning **me** to guard **me** in all **my** ways; they will lift me up in their hands so that **I** will not strike **my** foot against a stone.*
Psalm 91: 11-12

*He will command his angels concerning **me** to guard **me** carefully.*
Luke 4:10

My Anger...

Fools give full vent to their rage, but the wise bring calm in the end.
Proverbs 29:11

***I** should be quick to listen, slow to speak, and slow to become angry because **my** anger does not produce the righteousness that God desires.*
James 1: 19-20

Let my conversation be always full of grace, seasoned with salt, so that I may know how to answer everyone.
Colossians 4:6

*Tremble and do not sin; when **I** am in **my** bed, **I** should search **my** heart and be silent.*
Psalm 4:4

A hot-tempered person stirs up conflict, but the one who is patient calms a quarrel.
Proverbs 15:18

*Do not slander one another. When **I** speak against **my** brother or sister or judge them, then **I** speak against the law and judge it....there is only one Lawgiver and Judge, the one who is able to save and destroy. But **me** -who am **I** to judge **my** neighbor?*
James 4: 11-12

*Do not be quickly provoked in **my** spirit, for anger resides in the lap of fools.*
Ecclesiastes 7:9

My Attitude...

Rejoice always, pray continually, give thanks in all circumstances; for this is God's will for me in Christ Jesus. Do not quench the Spirit. Do not treat prophecies with contempt but test them all; hold on to what is good, reject every kind of evil.
1 Thessalonians 5:16-22

*Since, then, **I** have been raised with Christ, set **my** heart on things above, where Christ is, seated at the right hand of God. Set **my** mind on things above, not on earthly things.*
Colossians 3:1-2

*Finally, brothers and sisters, whatever is true, whatever is noble, whatever is right, whatever is pure, whatever is lovely, whatever is admirable - if anything is excellent or praiseworthy - think about such things. Whatever **I** have learned or received or heard from **him**, or seen in **him** - put it into practice. And the God of peace will be with **me**.*
Philippians 4:8-9

*But now **I** must also rid **myself** of all such things as these: anger, rage, malice, slander, and filthy language from **my** lips. As God's chosen, holy and dearly loved, **I** should clothe **myself** with compassion, kindness, humility, gentleness and patience. Bear with others and forgive others if **I** have a grievance against someone. Forgive as the Lord forgave **me**. And over all these virtues put on love, which binds them all together in perfect unity.*
Colossians 3:8, 12, 13 & 14

My Battle...

*He is **my** refuge in the day of disaster.*
Jeremiah 17:17b

*Be alert and of sober mind. **My** enemy the devil prowls around like a roaring lion looking for someone to devour. Resist him, standing firm in the faith.*
1 Peter 5: 8-9a

Sovereign Lord, my strong deliverer, you shield my head in the day of battle.
Psalm 140:7

Pray in the Spirit on all occasions with all kinds of prayers and requests. With this in mind, be alert and always keep on praying for all the Lord's people!

Ephesians 6:18

*Do not be afraid or discouraged because of this vast army. For the battle is not **mine**, but God's. **I** will not have to fight this battle. Take up **my** positions; stand firm and see the deliverance the Lord will give me. Do not be afraid; do not be discouraged. Go out to face them tomorrow, and the Lord will be with **me**.*

2 Chronicles 20: 15b & 17

*Put on the full armor of God so that I can stand against the devil's schemes. **My** struggle is not against flesh and blood, but against the rulers, against the authorities, against the powers of this dark world and against the spiritual forces of evil in the heavenly realms. Therefore, **I** need to put on the full armor of God, so that when evil comes, **I** may stand **my** ground.*

Ephesians 6: 11-13

My Balance...

Whoever fears God will avoid all extremes.

Ecclesiastes 7:18b

The wisdom of the prudent is to give thought to their ways, but the folly of fools is deception.

Proverbs 14:8

...for receiving instruction in prudent behavior, doing what is right and just and fair; for giving prudence to those who are simple, knowledge and discretion to the young.
Proverbs 1:3-4

Moses' father-in-law replied, "What you are doing is not good. You and these people who come to you will only wear yourselves out. The work is too heavy for you; you cannot handle it alone. Listen now to me and I will give you some advice, and may God be with you. You must be the people's representative before God and bring their disputes to him."
Exodus 18:17-19

My Beauty...

*...to bestow on **me** a crown of beauty instead of ashes, the oil of joy instead of mourning, and a garment of praise instead of a spirit of despair.*
Isaiah 61:3

*For **I** am God's handiwork, created in Christ Jesus to do good works, which God prepared in advance for **me** to do.*
Ephesians 2:10

Let the king be enthralled by your beauty; honor him, for he is your lord.
Psalm 45:11

But the Lord said to Samuel, "Do not consider his appearance or his height, for I have rejected him. The Lord does not look at the things people look at. People look at the outward appearance, but the Lord looks at the heart."
1 Samuel 16:7

For the Lord takes delight in his people; he crowns the humble with victory.
Psalm 149:4

Charm is deceptive, and beauty is fleeting; but a woman who fears the Lord is to be praised.
Proverbs 31:30

My Body...

*Do **I** not know that **my** body is a temple of the Holy Spirit, who is in **me**, whom **I** have received from God? **I** am not **my** own.*
1 Corinthians 6:19a

*Do not be wise in **my** own eyes; fear the Lord and shun evil. This will bring health to **my** body and nourishment to **my** bones!*
Proverbs 3:7-8

*"I have the right to do anything," you say - but not everything is beneficial. "I have the right to do anything" - but I will not be mastered by anything. You say, "Food for the stomach and the stomach for food, and God will destroy them both." The body, however, is not meant for sexual immorality but for the Lord...Do **I** not know that **my** body is a member of Christ Himself?*
1 Corinthians 6:12-15a

*I do not need to lose heart. Though outwardly **I** am wasting away, yet inwardly **I** am being renewed day by day.*
2 Corinthians 4:16

*So **I** fix my eyes not on what is seen, but on what is unseen, since what is seen is temporary, but what is unseen is eternal.*
2 Corinthians 4:18

How lovely is your dwelling place, Lord Almighty!
Psalm 84:1

My Bondage...

Set me free from my prison, that I may praise your name. Then the righteous will gather about me because of your goodness to me.
Psalm 142:7

*I will cry for help, and he will say: Here am I. "If **I** do away with the yoke of oppression, with the pointing finger and malicious talk, and if **I** spend **myself** on behalf of the hungry and satisfy the needs of the oppressed, then **my** light will rise in the darkness, and **my** night will become like the noonday. The LORD will guide **me** always; he will satisfy **my** needs in a sun-scorched land and will strengthen my frame. I will be like a well-watered garden, like a spring whose waters never fail."*
Isaiah 58:9b-11

...and provide for those who grieve in Zion - to bestow on them a crown of beauty instead of ashes, the oil of joy instead of mourning, and a garment of praise instead of a spirit of despair. They will be called oaks of righteousness, a planting of the Lord for the display of his splendor.
Isaiah 61:3

*But do not be afraid of them; remember well what the Lord **my** God did...I saw with **my** own eyes...the mighty hand and outstretched arm with which the Lord **my** God brought out!*
Deuteronomy 7:18-19a

*...he brought **me** out of Egypt by his Presence and his great strength.*
Deuteronomy 4:37b

My Boundaries...

LORD, you alone are my portion and my cup; you make my lot secure. The boundary lines have fallen for me in pleasant places; surely I have a delightful inheritance.
Psalm 16:5-6

You will find that I have planned no evil; my mouth has not transgressed.
Psalm 17:3b

My Calling...

When injustice has come my way, I later become passionate about others receiving the same form of injustice. Should I act upon the injustice I am passionate about? If I have opportunity and the gifts from God that are required for us to act, then yes – I should act, and if I do so...and tell us if I should act for the sake of those who have been treated unjustly then...He will guide me, answer me, and be my rearguard.
Isaiah 58:6-11 (paraphrased by Diane Pearce)

For God's gifts and his call are irrevocable.
Romans 11:29

Blessed are those who have regard for the weak; the LORD delivers them in times of trouble.
Psalm 41:1

Learn to do right; seek justice. Defend the oppressed. Take up the cause of the fatherless; plead the case of the widow.
Isaiah 1:17

Let the morning bring me word of your unfailing love, for I have put my trust in you. Show me the way I should go, for to you I entrust my life.
Psalm 143:8

Again Jesus said, "Peace be with you! As the Father has sent me, I am sending you."
John 20:21

I know that the Lord secures justice for the poor and upholds the cause of the needy.
Psalm 140:12

"The Spirit of the Lord is on me, because he has anointed me to proclaim good news to the poor. He has sent me to proclaim freedom for the prisoners and recovery of sight for the blind, to set the oppressed free, to proclaim the year of the Lord's favor."
Luke 4:18-19

*I need to commit **my** way to the Lord; trust in him and he will do this.*
Psalm 37:5

*His divine power has given **me** everything **I** need for a godly life through **my** knowledge of him who called **me** by his own glory and goodness. Through these he has given **me** his very great and precious promises, so that through them **I** may participate in the divine nature, having escaped the corruption in the world caused by evil desires.*

2 Peter 1:3-4

My Child...

My prayer is that I am used by God as a protector, provider, and eventually mentor to my child. I should consistently provide discipline so that they can discipline themselves as an adult. Never should I do for my child what he or she can do for themselves, so that I do not enable an unhealthy dependency on me. I should always verbalize my belief in their potential. They need to be independent of me and wholly dependent on God, His mercy, and His ways.

Diane Pearce

*Do not be afraid...He will pour out His Spirit on **my** offspring, and His blessing on **my** descendents.*

Isaiah 44:2b-3

"Restrain your voice from weeping and my eyes from tears, for my work will be rewarded," declares the LORD. "They will return from the land of the enemy. So there is hope for your descendants," declares the LORD. "Your children will return to their own land."

Jeremiah 31: 16-17

No discipline seems pleasant at the time, but painful. Later on, however, it produces a harvest of righteousness and peace for those who have been trained by it.
Hebrews 12:11

Start children off on the way they should go, and even when they are old they will not turn from it.
Proverbs 22:6

Folly is bound up in the heart of a child, but the rod of discipline will drive it far away.
Proverbs 22:15

...for each one should carry their own load.
Galatians 6:5

My son, do not forget my teaching, but keep my commands in your heart, for they will prolong your life many years and bring you peace and prosperity. Let love and faithfulness never leave you; bind them around your neck, write them on the tablet of your heart. Then you will win favor and a good name in the sight of God and man.
Proverbs 3:1-4

For even when we were with you, we gave you this rule: "The one who is unwilling to work shall not eat."
2 Thessalonians 3:10

My Comfort...

*Yet the Lord longs to be gracious to **me**; therefore he will rise up to show **me** compassion. For the LORD is a God of justice. Blessed are all who wait for him!*
Isaiah 30:18

The moon will shine like the sun, and the sunlight will be seven times brighter, like the light of seven full days, when the LORD binds up the bruises of his people and heals the wounds he inflicted.
Isaiah 30:26

Shout for joy, you heavens; rejoice, you earth; burst into song, you mountains! For the Lord comforts his people and will have compassion on his afflicted ones.
Isaiah 49:13

*He is the one who comforts **me**. Who am **I** that **I** fear mere mortals, human beings who are but grass, that I forget the LORD **my** Maker, who stretches out the heavens and who lays the foundations of the earth, that **I** live in constant terror every day because of the wrath of the oppressor, who is bent on destruction? For where is the wrath of the oppressor?*
Isaiah 51: 12-13

*Because of the Lord's great love **I** am not consumed, for his compassions never fail.*
Lamentations 3:22

You who are my Comforter in sorrow, my heart is faint within me.
Jeremiah 8:18

Surely God is good to Israel, to those who are pure in heart. But as for me, my feet had almost slipped; I had nearly lost my foothold.
Psalm 73:1-2

As for me, I will always have hope; I will praise you more and more. My mouth will tell of your righteous deeds, of your saving acts all day long -though I know not how to relate them all.
Psalm 71:14-15

My Communication with Others...

*Accept one another, then, just as Christ has accepted **me**, in order to bring praise to God.*
Romans 15:7

*Do not judge, and **I** will not be judged. Do not condemn, and **I** will not be condemned. Forgive, and **I** will be forgiven. Give, and it will be given to **me**. A good measure, pressed down, shaken together and running over, will be poured into **my** lap. For with the measure **I** use, it will be measured to **me**.*
Luke 6: 37-38

Whoever of you loves life and desires to see many good days, keep your tongue from evil and your lips from telling lies.
Psalm 34:12-13

I said, "I will watch my ways and keep my tongue from sin; I will put a muzzle on my mouth while in the presence of the wicked."
Psalm 39:1

Therefore the prudent keep quiet in such times, for the times are evil.
Amos 5:13

Set a guard over my mouth, Lord; keep watch over the door of my lips.
Psalm 141:3

My Confidence...

*Have no fear of sudden disaster or of the ruin that overtakes the wicked, for the LORD will be at **my** side and will keep **my** foot from being snared.*
Proverbs 3:25-26

You armed me with strength for battle.
Psalm 18:39

The Lord is the stronghold of my life - of whom shall I be afraid?
Psalm 27:1b

For you have been my hope, Sovereign Lord, my confidence since my youth. From birth I have relied on you; you brought me forth from my mother's womb. I will ever praise you.
Psalm 71:5-6

When I called, you answered me; you greatly emboldened me.
Psalm 138:3

The LORD will vindicate me; your love, LORD, endures forever - do not abandon the works of your hands.
Psalm 138:8

*Get **myself** ready! Stand up and say to them whatever He commands **me**. Do not be terrified by them, or **He** will terrify **me** before them.*
Jeremiah 1:17

*Let someone else praise **me**, and not **my** own mouth; an outsider, and not **my** own lips.*
Proverbs 27:2

*Such confidence **I** have through Christ before God. Not that **I** am competent in **myself** to claim anything for **myself**, but **my** competence comes from God.*
2 Corinthians 3:4-5

Cursed is the one whose trust is in man, who draws strength from mere flesh and whose heart turns away from the LORD.
Jeremiah 17:5

But blessed is the one who trusts is in the LORD, whose confidence is in Him.
Jeremiah 17:7

My Critics...

*Hear **Him**, **I** who know what is right, **I** have taken His instruction to heart: Do not fear the reproach of mere mortals or be terrified by their insults.*
Isaiah 51:7

He has put **His** words in **my** mouth and covered **me** with the shadow of **His** hand - **He** who set the heavens in place, who laid the foundations of the earth.
Isaiah 51:16

Though I walk in the midst of trouble, you preserve my life. You stretch out your hand against the anger of my foes; with your right hand you save me.
Psalm 138:7

Who will bring any charge against those whom God has chosen? It is God who justifies. Who then is the one who condemns? No one.
Romans 8:33-34a

My Defender...

The LORD is my light and my salvation - whom shall I fear? The LORD is the stronghold of my life - of whom shall I be afraid? When the wicked advance against me to devour me, it is my enemies and my foes who will stumble and fall. Though an army besiege me, my heart will not fear; though war break out against me, even then I will be confident.
Psalm 27:1-3

Defend the weak and the fatherless; uphold the cause of the poor and the oppressed. Rescue the weak and the needy; deliver them from the hand of the wicked.
Psalm 82: 3-4

Though I walk in the midst of trouble, you preserve my life. You stretch out your hand against the anger of my foes; with your right hand you save me.
Psalm 138:7

He defends the cause of the fatherless.
Deuteronomy 10:18

My Delivery...

Sovereign LORD, my strong deliverer, you shield my head in the day of battle. Do not grant the wicked their desires, LORD; do not let their plans succeed.
Psalm 140:7-8

Heal me, LORD, and I will be healed; save me and I will be saved, for you are the one that I praise.
Jeremiah 17:14

You are my refuge in the day of disaster!
Jeremiah 17:17

My Despair...

*(He provides for me when I grieve)...to bestow on **me** a crown of beauty instead of ashes, the oil of joy instead of mourning, and a garment of praise instead of a spirit of despair. I will be called an oak of righteousness, a planting of the LORD for the display of his splendor.*
Isaiah 61:3

*Many, LORD, are asking, "Who will bring us prosperity?" Let the light of your face shine on **me**.*
Psalm 4:6

In peace I will lie down and sleep, for you alone, LORD, make me dwell in safety.
Psalm 4:8

The LORD is a refuge for the oppressed, a stronghold in times of trouble.
Psalm 9:9

*Praise the LORD, my soul, and forget not all his benefits...who redeems **my** life from the pit and crowns **me** with love and compassion, who satisfies **my** desires with good things so that **my** youth is renewed like the eagle's.*
Psalm 103: 2a, 4-5

*And **I** know that in all things God works for **my** good because **I** love him, **I** have been called according to His purpose.*
Romans 8:28

*If God is for **me**, who can be against **me**?*
Romans 8:31b

My Dignity...

***He** will walk with **me** and be **my** God, and **I** will be **His** people. **He** is the Lord **my** God, who brought **me** out of Egypt (slavery) so that I would no longer be a slave...**He** broke the bars of **my** yoke and enabled **me** to walk with **my** head held high.*
Leviticus 26: 12-13

*In a desert land he found **me**, in a barren and howling waste. He shielded **me** and cared for **me**; he guarded **me** as the apple of his eye, like an eagle that stirs up its nest and hovers over its young, that spreads its wings to catch them and carries them aloft. The LORD alone led **me**; no foreign god was with **me**.*
Deuteronomy 32:10-12

*Know that the LORD is God. It is he who made **me**, and **I** am his... the sheep of his pasture.*
Psalm 100:3

*I am clothed with strength and dignity; **I** can laugh at the days to come.*
Proverbs 31:25

My Discipline...

Blessed is the one whom God corrects; so do not despise the discipline of the Almighty. For he wounds, but he also binds up; he injures, but his hands also heal.
Job 5:17-18

*If **I** love discipline, **I** love knowledge, but if **I** hate correction **I'm** stupid.*
Proverbs 12:1

Diligent hands will rule, but laziness ends in forced labor.
Proverbs 12:24

*When **I** heed discipline **I** will show the way to life, but if **I** ignore correction **I** will lead others astray.*
Proverbs 10:17

*I am blessed when you discipline **me**, LORD, when you teach **me** from your law; you grant **me** relief from the days of trouble.*
Psalm 94: 12-13

Like a city whose walls are broken through is a person who lacks self-control.
Proverbs 25:28

For the Spirit God gave us does not make us timid, but gives us power, love and self-discipline.
2 Timothy 1:7

My Disappointments...

*What causes fights and quarrels? Don't they come from **my** desires that battle within **me**? I desire but do not have...I covet but I cannot get what I want, so I quarrel and fight. I do not have because I do not ask God. When I ask I do not receive, because I ask with wrong motives, that I may spend what I get on **my** pleasures.*
James 4:1-3

Why, my soul, are you downcast? Why so disturbed within me? Put your hope in God, for I will yet praise him, my Savior and my God.
Psalm 42:11

My Enemies...

*Surely **He** will deliver **me** for a good purpose; surely **He** will make **my** enemies plead with **me** in times of disaster and times of distress.*
Jeremiah 15:11

He will save me from the hands of the wicked and deliver me from the grasp of the cruel.
Jeremiah 15:21

...who saves me from my enemies. You exalted me above my foes; from a violent man you rescued me.
Psalm 18:48

May those who seek my life be disgraced and put to shame; may those who plot my ruin be turned back in dismay. May they be like chaff before the wind, with the angel of the Lord driving them away.
Psalm 35:4-5

The Lord is my light and my salvation—whom shall I fear? The Lord is the stronghold of my life—of whom shall I be afraid? When the wicked advance against me to devour me, it is my enemies and my foes who will stumble and fall. Though an army besiege me, my heart will not fear; though war break out against me, even then I will be confident.
Psalm 27:1-3

Through you we push back our enemies; through your name we trample our foes.
Psalm 44:5

I put no trust in my bow, my sword does not bring me victory; but you give us victory over our enemies, you put our adversaries to shame. In God we make our boast all day long, and we will praise your name forever.
Psalm 44:6-8

My Faith...

*Now faith is confidence in what **I** hope for and assurance about what **I** do not see.*
Hebrews 11:1

And without faith it is impossible to please God, because anyone who comes to him must believe that he exists and that he rewards those who earnestly seek him.
Hebrews 11:6

*Whatever **I** ask for in prayer, believe that **I** have received it, and it will be **mine**!*
Mark 11:24

Faith by itself, if it is not accompanied by action, is dead.
James 2:17

***My** faith will be made complete by what I do.*
James 2:22b

***I** am considered righteous by what **I** do and not by faith alone.*
James 2:24

*Call to **Him** and **He** will answer **me** and tell **me** great and unsearchable things that **I** do not know.*
Jeremiah 33:3

Consequently, faith comes from hearing the message, and the message is heard through the word about Christ.
Romans 10:17

By faith Abraham...obeyed and went, even though he did not know where he was going.
Hebrews 11:8

And by faith even Sarah...was enabled to bear children because she considered him faithful who had made the promise.
Hebrews 11:11

*According to **my** faith let it be done to **me**.*
Matthew 9:29b

My Family...

*I must not worship the LORD **my** God in their way. But **I am** to seek the place the LORD **my** God will choose from among all **my** tribes to put his Name there for his dwelling. To that place **I** must go; there bring **my** burnt offerings and sacrifices, **my** tithes and special gifts, what **I** have vowed to give and **my** freewill offerings, and the firstborn of **my** herds and flocks. There, in the presence of the LORD **my** God, **me** and **my** family shall eat and shall rejoice in everything **I** have put **my** hand to, because the LORD **my** God has blessed **me**.*
Deuteronomy 12: 4-7

God sets the lonely in families, he leads out the prisoners with singing,
Psalm 68:6a

*He has prayed for **me**...that **my** faith may not fail. And when **I** have turned back, **I** should strengthen others.*
Luke 22:32

Love must be sincere. Hate what is evil; cling to what is good. Be devoted to one another in love. Honor others above **myself***. Never be lacking in zeal, but keep* **my** *spiritual fervor, serving the Lord. Be joyful in hope, patient in affliction, faithful in prayer. Share with the Lord's people who are in need. Practice hospitality. Bless those who persecute* **me***; bless and do not curse. Rejoice with those who rejoice; mourn with those who mourn. Live in harmony with one another. Do not be proud, but be willing to associate with people of low position. Do not be conceited. Do not repay anyone evil for evil. Be careful to do what is right in the eyes of everyone.*

Romans 12:9-17

My Fears...

Hear me, you who know what is right, you people who have taken my instruction to heart: Do not fear the reproach of mere mortals or be terrified by their insults.

Isaiah 51:7

And even the very hairs of **my** *head are all numbered. So* **I** *should not be afraid;* **I** *am worth more than many sparrows.*

Matthew 10: 30-31

What I feared has come upon me; what I dreaded has happened to me. I have no peace, no quietness; I have no rest, but only turmoil.

Job 3:25-26

He *will instruct* **me** *and teach* **me** *in the way* **I** *should go;* **He** *will counsel* **me** *with* **His** *loving eye on* **me***.*

Psalm 32:8

*...but the LORD's unfailing love surrounds **me** when **I** trust in him.*
Psalm 32:10b

*...because God has said, "Never will **He** leave **me**; never will He forsake **me**." So **I** say with confidence, "The Lord is **my** helper; **I** will not be afraid. What can mere mortals do to **me**?"*
Hebrews 13:5b-6

*"Do not fear, for **He** has redeemed **me**; **He** has summoned **me** by name; **I** am **His**. **I** am precious and honored in **His** sight and **He** loves **me**.*
Isaiah 43:1b,4a

*Do not be terrified by them, for the LORD **my** God, who is with me, is a great and awesome God.*
Deuteronomy 7:21

My Friendships...

Carry each other's burdens and in this way you will fulfill the law of Christ.
Galatians 6:2

I should not become conceited, provoking and envying others.
Galatians 5:26

*Finally, all of you, be like-minded, be sympathetic, love one another, be compassionate and humble. Do not repay evil with evil, or insult with insult. On the contrary, repay evil with blessing, because to this **I** was called so that **I** may inherit a blessing.*
1 Peter 3:8-10

Light in a messenger's eyes brings joy to the heart, and good news gives health to the bones.
Proverbs 15:30

Do not be misled: "Bad company corrupts good character."
1 Corinthians 15:33

*...guard what has been entrusted to **my** care. Turn away from godless chatter.*
1 Timothy 6:20

*Don't have anything to do with foolish and stupid arguments, because **I** know they produce quarrels. And the Lord's servant must not be quarrelsome but must be kind to everyone, able to teach, not resentful.*
2 Timothy 2:23-24

The one whose walk is blameless, who does what is righteous, who speaks the truth from their heart; whose tongue utters no slander, who does no wrong to a neighbor, and casts no slur on others; who despises a vile person but honors those who fear the LORD; who keeps an oath even when it hurts, and does not change their mind; who lends money to the poor without interest; who does not accept a bribe against the innocent.
Psalm 15:2-5

My God...

*For **He** is the LORD **my** God, who stirs up the sea so that its waves roar - the LORD Almighty is his name.*
Isaiah 51:15

*Who am I, that I fear mere mortals ... that I forget the LORD, **my** maker, who stretches out the heavens and who lays the foundations of the earth.*
Isaiah 51:12b-13

...the Lord, the compassionate and gracious God, slow to anger, abounding in love and faithfulness, maintaining love to thousands, and forgiving wickedness, rebellion, and sin. Yet he does not leave the guilty unpunished; he punishes the children and their children for the sin of the parents to the third and fourth generation.
Exodus 34:6-7

My Grief...

The righteous perish, and no one takes it to heart; the devout are taken away, and no one understands that the righteous are taken away to be spared from evil. Those who walk uprightly enter into peace.
Isaiah 57:1-2

*Do not grieve, for the joy of the Lord is **my** strength.*
Nehemiah 8:10b

The LORD is close to the brokenhearted and saves those who are crushed in spirit.
Psalm 34:18

My Guardrails...

***His** statutes are my heritage forever; they are the joy of my heart.*
Psalm 119:111

*Religion that God our Father accepts as pure and faultless is this: to look after orphans and widows in their distress and to keep **myself** from being polluted by the world.*

James 1:27

*Above all else, **I** need to guard **my** heart, for everything **I** do flows from it. Keep **my** mouth free of perversity; keep corrupt talk far from **my** lips. Let **my** eyes look straight ahead; fix **my** gaze directly before me. Give careful thought to the paths for **my** feet and be steadfast in all **my** ways. Do not turn to the right or the left; keep **my** feet from evil.*

Proverbs 4:23-27

*I will know that **He** is the LORD, when **He** deals with **me** for **His** name's sake and not according to **my** evil ways and **my** corrupt practices.*

Ezekiel 20:44

My Guide...

*But seek first his kingdom and his righteousness, and all these things will be given to **me** as well.*

Matthew 6:33

You will find that I have planned no evil; my mouth has not transgressed.

Psalm 17:3b

May these words of my mouth and this meditation of my heart be pleasing in your sight, LORD, my Rock and my Redeemer!

Psalm 19:14

You are God, my stronghold…Send me your light and your faithful care, let them lead me; let them bring me to your holy mountain, to the place where you dwell.

Psalm 43: 2-3

I am sent out like sheep among the wolves. Therefore I need to be shrewd as a snake, yet innocent as a dove.

Matthew 10:16

So is His word that comes out from His mouth: It will not return to Him empty, but will accomplish what He desires and achieve the purpose for which He sent it.

Isaiah 55:11

Since you are my rock and my fortress, for the sake of your name lead and guide me.

Psalm 31:3

For this God is our God forever and ever; he will be our guide even to the end.

Psalm 48:14

My Guilt...

If I repent, He will restore me that I may serve Him; if I utter worthy, not worthless, words, I will be His spokesman.

Jeremiah 15:19

Search me, God, and know my heart; test me and know my anxious thoughts. See if there is any offensive way in me, and lead me in the way everlasting.

Psalm 139:23-24

Blessed is the one whose transgressions are forgiven, whose sins are covered. Blessed is the one whose sin the LORD does not count against them and in whose spirit is no deceit.

Psalm 32:1-2

My Happiness...

The LORD is my strength and my shield; my heart trusts in him, and he helps me. My heart leaps for joy, and with my song I praise him.

Psalm 28:7

You turned my wailing into dancing; you removed my sackcloth and clothed me with joy, that my heart may sing your praises and not be silent. LORD my God, I will praise you forever.

Psalm 30:11-12

He lifted me out of the slimy pit, out of the mud and mire; he set my feet on a rock and gave me a firm place to stand. He put a new song in my mouth, a hymn of praise to our God. Many will see and fear the LORD and put their trust in him.

Psalm 40:2-3

But may the righteous be glad and rejoice before God; may they be happy and joyful.

Psalm 68:3

My Healing...

LORD my God, I called to you for help, and you healed me. You, LORD, brought me up from the realm of the dead; you spared me from going down to the pit.
Psalm 30:2-3

For he has not despised or scorned the suffering of the afflicted one; he has not hidden his face from him but has listened to his cry for help.
Psalm 22:24

I sought the LORD, and he answered me; he delivered me from all my fears. Those who look to him are radiant; their faces are never covered with shame.
Psalm 34:4-5

*The righteous cry out, and the LORD hears **me**; he delivers **me** from all **my** troubles.*
Psalm 34:17

My Heart...

Search me, God, and know my heart; test me and know my anxious thoughts. See if there is any offensive way in me, and lead me in the way everlasting.
Psalm 139:23-24

Do not let my heart be drawn to what is evil.
Psalm 141:4a

*Apply **my** heart to instruction and **my** ears to words of knowledge.*
Proverbs 23:12

*... give **Him my** heart and let **my** eyes delight in **His** ways.*
Proverbs 23:26

Create in me a pure heart, O God, and renew a steadfast spirit within me.
Psalm 51:10

Yet you desired faithfulness even in the womb; you taught me wisdom in that secret place.
Psalm 51:6

*As for **me**, if I walk before **Him** faithfully with integrity of heart and up-rightness...and do all **He** commands and observe **His** decrees and laws, **He** will establish **my** (place).*
1 Kings 9:4-5

*Above all else, guard **my** heart, for everything **I** do flows from it. Keep **my** mouth free of perversity; keep corrupt talk far from **my** lips. Let **my** eyes look straight ahead; fix **my** gaze directly before **me**. Give careful thought to the path for **my** feet and be steadfast in all **my** ways. Do not turn to the right or the left; keep my feet from evil.*
Proverbs 4:23-27

He will bring to light what is hidden in darkness and will expose the motives of the heart. At that time each will receive their praise from God.
1 Corinthians 4:5b

My Help...

The LORD is my strength and my shield; my heart trusts in him, and he helps me. My heart leaps for joy, and with my song I praise him.
Psalm 28:7

...you have been my helper. Do not reject me or forsake me, God my Savior.
Psalm 27:9b

...according to your love remember me, for you, LORD, are good.
Psalm 25:7b

*Now may the God of peace who...brought back from the dead our Lord Jesus...equip **me** with everything good for doing his will, and may he work in **me** what is pleasing to him.*
Hebrews 13:20-21

Because the Sovereign LORD helps me, I will not be disgraced. Therefore, have I set my face like flint, and I know I will not be put to shame.
Isaiah 50:7

*...he who began a good work in **me** will carry it on to completion.*
Philippians 1:6

*For **He** is the LORD **my** God who takes hold of **my** right hand and says to **me**, Do not fear; **He** will help me. Do not be afraid... do not fear, for **He himself** will help **me**, declares the LORD, **my** Redeemer, the Holy One of Israel...so that people may see and know, may consider and understand, that the hand of the LORD has done this, that the Holy One of Israel has created it.*
Isaiah 41:13-14, 20

*This is what the Lord says – He who made **me**, who formed **me** in the womb, and who will help **me**: Do not be afraid.*
Isaiah 44:2a

But you, God, see the trouble of the afflicted; you consider my grief and take it in hand. The victims commit themselves to you; you are the helper of the fatherless.
Psalm 10:14

...defending the fatherless and the oppressed, so that mere earthly mortals will never again strike terror.
Psalm 10:18

My Hope...

Put your hope in God, for I will yet praise him, my Savior and my God.
Psalm 42:5b, 11b & Psalm 43:5b

Yes, my soul, find rest in God; my hope comes from Him. Truly he is my rock and my salvation; he is my fortress, I will not be shaken.
Psalm 62:5-6

May those who fear you rejoice when they see me, for I have put my hope in your word.
Psalm 119:74

...the LORD delights in those who fear him, who put their hope in his unfailing love.
Psalm 147:11

...but those who hope in the LORD will renew their strength. They will soar on wings like eagles; they will run and not grow weary, they will walk and not be faint.
Isaiah 40:31

*I have this hope that is an anchor for **my** soul, firm and secure.*
Hebrews 6:19

*God is not unjust; he will not forget **my** work and the love **I** have shown him as **I** helped his people and continue to help them. **I** need to show this same diligence to the very end, so that what **I** hope for may be fully realized. **I** should not become lazy, but imitate those who through faith and patience inherit what has been promised.*
Hebrews 6:10-12

Now faith is confidence in what I hope for and assurance about what I do not see.
Hebrews 11:1

*For everything that was written in the past was written to teach me, so that through the endurance taught in the Scriptures and the encouragement they provide **I** might have hope.*
Romans 15:4

*Because of the LORD's great love, **I** am not consumed, for his compassions never fail. They are new every morning; great is your faithfulness. I say to myself, "The LORD is my portion; therefore I will wait for him. The Lord is good to **me** because **my** hope is in him, because **I** seek him.*
Lamentations 3:22-25

As for me, I will always have hope; I will praise you more and more. My mouth will tell of your righteous deeds, of your saving acts all day long - though I know not how to relate them all.
Psalm 71:14-15

My Humility...

He guides the humble in what is right and teaches them his way.
Psalm 25:9

*Never again will **I** be haughty on **his** holy hill. But **he** will leave within **me** the meek and humble. The remnant of Israel will trust in the name of the LORD.*
Zephaniah 3:11b-12

He saves the humble but brings low those whose eyes are haughty.
Psalm 18:27

Do not keep talking so proudly or let your mouth speak such arrogance, for the LORD is a God who knows, and by him deeds are weighed.
1 Samuel 2:3

My Hurt...

Joseph speaking to his brothers who had grossly mistreated him: "So then, it was not you who sent me here, but God." Joseph then returned blessings to his brother who had persecuted him.
Genesis 45:8

You intended to harm me, but God intended it for good to accomplish what is now being done...So then, don't be afraid.
Genesis 50:20-21a

"Joseph is a fruitful vine...With bitterness archers attacked him; they shot at him with hostility. But his bow remained steady, his strong arms stayed limber, because of the hand of the Mighty One of Jacob, because of the Shepherd, the Rock of Israel, because of your father's God, who helps you, because of the Almighty who blesses you with blessings of the skies above, blessings of the deep springs below, blessings of the breast and womb."
Genesis 49:22-25

In fact, everyone who wants to live a godly life in Christ Jesus will be persecuted.
2 Timothy 3:12

Make every effort to live in peace with everyone and to be holy; without holiness no one will see the Lord. See to it that no one falls short of the grace of God and that no bitter root grows up to cause trouble and defile many.
Hebrews 12:14-15

And we know that in all things God works for the good of those who love him, who have been called according to his purpose.
Romans 8:28

I called on your name, LORD, from the depths of the pit. You heard my plea: "Do not close your ears to my cry for relief." You came near when I called you, and you said, "Do not fear." You, Lord took up my case; you redeemed my life. LORD, you have seen the wrong done to me. Uphold my cause.
Lamentations 3:55-59

But you, God, see the trouble of the afflicted; you consider their grief and take it in hand. The victims commit themselves to you; you are the helper of the fatherless.
Psalm 10:14

Though you have made me see troubles, many and bitter, you will restore my life again; from the depths of the earth you will again bring me up. You will increase my honor and comfort me once more.
Psalm 71:20-21

This day is holy to our Lord. Do not grieve, for the joy of the LORD is my strength..."Be still, for this is a holy day. Do not grieve.
Nehemiah 8:10b & 11b

...he will remove his people's disgrace from all the earth.
Isaiah 25:8b

My Identity...

For you created my inmost being; you knit me together in my mother's womb. I praise you because I am fearfully and wonderfully made; your works are wonderful, I know that full well.
Psalm 139:13-14

You greatly emboldened me.
Psalm 138:3b

From birth I was cast on you; from my mother's womb you have been my God.
Psalm 22:10

My Integrity...

"Woe to him who builds his palace by unrighteousness, his upper rooms by injustice, making his own people work for nothing, not paying them for their labor."
Jeremiah 22:13

Dishonest money dwindles away, but whoever gathers money little by little makes it grow.
Proverbs 13:11

See, the enemy is puffed up; his desires are not upright - but the righteous person will live by his faithfulness.
Habakkuk 2:4

My Jealousy...

*But if **I** harbor bitter envy and selfish ambition in **my** heart, do not boast about it or deny the truth. Such "wisdom" does not come down from heaven but is earthly, unspiritual, and of the devil. For where you have envy and selfish ambition, there you find disorder and every evil practice.*
James 3:14-16

*Fear the LORD, you his holy people, for those who fear him lack noth-
ing.*
Psalm 34:9

*Be still before the LORD and wait patiently for him; do not fret when
people succeed in their ways, when they carry out their wicked schemes.*
Psalm 37:7

*Do not be overawed when others grow rich, when the splendor of their
houses increases.*
Psalm 49:16

My Justice...

For the LORD is a God of retribution; he will repay in full.
Jeremiah 51:56b

*And will not God bring about justice for his chosen ones, who cry out to
him day and night? Will He keep putting them off? I tell you, he will see
that they get justice, and quickly.*
Luke 18:7-8

*Do not say, "I will pay you back for this wrong!" Wait for the LORD, and
he will avenge me.*
Proverbs 20:22

*I know that the LORD secures justice for the poor and upholds the cause
of the needy.*
Psalm 140:12

In faithfulness he will bring forth justice; he will not falter or be discouraged till he establishes justice on earth.
Isaiah 42:3b-4a

You, Lord, took up my case; you redeemed my life. LORD, you have seen the wrong done to me. Uphold my cause!
Lamentations 3:58-59

Do not take revenge, my dear friends, but leave room for God's wrath for it is written: "It is mine to avenge; I will repay," says the LORD. On the contrary: "If your enemy is hungry, feed him; if he is thirsty, give him something to drink. In doing this, you will heap burning coals on his head."
Romans 12:19-20

For the LORD is righteous, he loves justice; the upright will see his face. Psalm 11:7Vindicate me, my God, and plead my cause against an unfaithful nation. Rescue me from those who are deceitful and wicked.
Psalm 43:1

Let my vindication come from you; may your eyes see what is right.
Psalm 17:2

Do not drag me away with the wicked, with those who do evil, who speak cordially with their neighbors but harbor malice in their hearts. Repay them for their deeds and for their evil work; repay them for what their hands have done and bring back on them what they deserve. Because they have no regard for the deeds of the LORD and what his hands have done, he will tear them down and never build them up again.
Psalm 28:3-5

*He will contend with those who contend with **me**, and **my** children **he** will save. **He** will make **my** oppressors eat their own flesh; they will be drunk on their own blood, as with wine. Then all mankind will know that **He**, the LORD, is **my** Savior, **my** Reedeemer, the Mighty One of Jacob.*
Isaiah 49: 25b-26

The LORD will defend my cause and avenge me.
Jeremiah 51:36b

*He will repay **me** for the years the locusts have eaten...**His** great army was sent to **me**. I will have plenty to eat, until **I** am full, and **I** will praise the name of the LORD **my** God, who has worked wonders for **me**; never again will **His** people be shamed. Then **I** will know that **He** is in Israel, that **He** is the LORD **my** God, and that there is no other; never again will **His** people be shamed.*
Joel 2:25-27

Woe to him who builds his house by unjust gain, setting his nest on high to escape the clutches of ruin! You have plotted the ruin of many peoples, shaming your own house and forfeiting your life.
Habakkuk 2:9-10

My Legacy...

Only be careful, and watch yourselves closely so that you do not forget the things your eyes have seen or let them fade from your heart as long as you live. Teach them to your children and to their children after them.
Deuteronomy 4:9

Acknowledge and take to heart this day that the Lord is God in heaven above and on the earth below. There is no other. Keep his decrees and commands, which I am giving you today, so that it may go well with you and your children after you and that you may live long in the land the Lord your God gives you for all time.
Deuteronomy 4:39-40

Yet the Lord set his affection on your ancestors and loved them, and he chose you, their descendants, above all the nations - as it is today. Circumcise your hearts, therefore, and do not be stiff-necked any longer.
Deuteronomy 10:15-16

My Marriage...

But since sexual immorality is occurring, each man should have sexual relations with his own wife, and each woman with her own husband.
1 Corinthians 7:2

The wife does not have authority over her own body but yields it to her husband. In the same way, the husband does not have authority over his own body but yields it to his wife. Do not deprive each other except perhaps by mutual consent and for a time, so that you may devote your-selves to prayer. Then come together again so that Satan will not tempt you because of your lack of self control. I say this as a concession, not as a command.
1 Corinthians 7:4-6

Carry each other's burdens, and in this way we will fulfill the law of Christ.
Galatians 6:2

Submit to one another out of reverence for Christ. Now as the church submits to Christ, so also wives should submit to their husbands in everything. However, each one of you also must love his wife as he loves himself, and the wife must respect her husband.
Ephesians 5:21, 24, & 33

Therefore if I have any encouragement from being united with Christ, if any comfort from his love, if any common sharing in the Spirit, if any tenderness and compassion, then make my joy complete by being like-minded, having the same love, being one in spirit and of one mind. Do nothing out of selfish ambition or vain conceit. Rather, in humility value others above **myself***, not looking to* **my** *own interests but to the interests of the others.*
Philippians 2:1-4

My Mentoring...

Stand up in the presence of the aged, show respect for the elderly and revere your God.
Leviticus 19:32

Be shepherds of God's flock that is under your care, watching over them—not because you must, but because you are willing, as God wants you to be; not pursuing dishonest gain, but eager to serve; not lording it over those entrusted to you, but being examples to the flock. And when the Chief Shepherd appears, you will receive the crown of glory that will never fade away. In the same way, you who are younger, submit yourselves to your elders. All of you, clothe yourselves with humility toward one another because, "God opposes the proud but shows favor to the humble." Humble yourselves, therefore, under God's mighty hand, that he may lift you up in due time. Cast all your anxiety on him because he cares for you.
1 Peter 5:2-7

My Mercy...

For if I forgive other people when they sin against me, my heavenly Father will also forgive me. But if I do not forgive others their sins, my Father will not forgive my sins.
Matthew 6:14-15

Do not judge, or I too will be judged. For in the same way I judge others, I will be judged, and with the measure I use, it will be measured to me.
Matthew 7:1-2

So in everything, do to others what I would have them do to me, for this sums up the Law and the Prophets.
Matthew 7:12

My Money...

A generous person will prosper; whoever refreshes others will be refreshed!
Proverbs 11:25

Those who trust in their riches will fall, but the righteous will thrive like a green leaf.
Proverbs 11:28

But godliness with contentment is great gain. I brought nothing into the world, and I can take nothing out of it. But if I have food and clothing, I should be content with that. Those who want to get rich fall into temptation and a trap and into many foolish and harmful desires that plunge them into ruin and destruction.
1 Timothy 6:6-9

My Mouth...

You have put your words in my mouth and covered me with the shadow of your hand.
Isaiah 51:16

The words of the reckless pierce like a swords, but the tongue of the wise brings healing.
Proverbs 12:18

Truthful lips endure forever, but a lying tongue lasts only a moment.
Proverbs 12:19

If I guard my lips I guard my life but if I speak rashly I will come to ruin.
Proverbs 13:3

May these words of my mouth and this mediation of my heart be pleasing in your sight, LORD, my Rock and my Redeemer.
Psalm 19:14

Set a guard over my mouth, LORD; keep watch over the door of my lips.
Psalm 141:3

*Keep **my** tongue from evil and **my** lips from telling lies. Turn from evil and do good; seek peace and pursue it. The eyes of the LORD are on the righteous, and his ears are attentive to their cry; but the face of the LORD is against those who do evil, to blot out their name from the earth. The righteous cry out, and the LORD hears them; he delivers them from all their troubles.*
Psalm 34:13-17

I said, "I will watch my ways and keep my tongue from sin; I will put a

muzzle on my mouth while in the presence of the wicked."
Psalm 39:1

*For the sins of **my** mouth, for the words of **my** lips, let **me** be caught in **my** pride. For the curses and lies I utter, consume them in your wrath, consume them till they are no more.*
Psalm 59:12-13

My Obstacles...

You bring me back from captivity... so I may bring you renown, joy, praise and honor.
Jeremiah 33:7a, 9a

*But **He** will restore **me** to health and heal **my** wounds...because **I** am called an outcast...for whom no one cares.*
Jeremiah 30:17

To bestow on them a crown of beauty instead of ashes, the oil of joy instead of mourning, and a garment instead of a spirit of despair.
Isaiah 61:3

My Parent...

The victims commit themselves to you; you are the helper of the fatherless.
Psalm 10:14b

You, LORD, hear the desire of the afflicted; you encourage them, and you listen to their cry, defending the fatherless and the oppressed.
Psalm 10:17-18a

Though my father and mother forsake me, the LORD will receive me.
Psalm 27:10

*Though **my** mother may forget **me**, **He** will not forget **me**! See, **He** has engraved **me** on the palms of **His** hands.*
Isaiah 49:15b-16

He defends the cause of the fatherless.
Deuteronomy 10:18a

From birth I was cast upon you; from my mother's womb you have been my God.
Psalm 22:10

My Path...

Teach me your way, LORD; lead me in a straight path because of my oppressors.
Psalm 27:11

*He will lead **me** beside streams of water on a level path where **I** will not stumble.*
Jeremiah 31:9b

*For the LORD will go before **me**, the God of Israel will be **my** rear guard.*
Isaiah 52:12b

Do not let my heart be drawn to what is evil so that I take part in wicked deeds along with those who are evildoers; do not let me eat their delicacies.
Psalm 141:4

All the days ordained for me were written in your book before one of them came to be.
Psalm 139:16b

When my spirit grows faint within me, it is you who watch over my way. In the path where I walk people have hidden a snare for me. Look and see, there is no one at my right hand; no one is concerned for me. I have no refuge; no one cares for my life. I cry to you, LORD; I say, "You are my refuge, my portion in the land of the living."
Psalm 142:3-5

If I do not stand firm in my faith, I will not stand at all.
Isaiah 7:9b

*But as for **me**, **I** should continue in what **I** have learned and have been convinced of, because **I** know those from whom **I've** learned it, and how from infancy **I** have known the Holy Scriptures, which are able to make **me** wise for salvation through faith in Christ Jesus."*
2 Timothy 3:14-15

LORD, I know that people's lives are not their own; it is not for them to direct their steps.
Jeremiah 10:23

Show me your ways, LORD, teach me your paths. Guide me in your truth and teach me, for you are God my Savior, and my hope is in you all day long.
Psalm 25:4-5

My Peace...

"Submit to God and be at peace with him; in this way prosperity will come to you. Accept instruction from his mouth and lay up his words in your heart."
Job 22:21-22

*Peace **He** leaves with **me**; **His** peace **He** gives to **me**. **He** does not give to **me** as the world gives. Do not let my heart be troubled and do not be afraid.*
John 14:27

*Let the peace of Christ rule in **my** heart, since as members of one body I am called to peace. And be thankful. Let the message of Christ dwell richly in **me**.*
Colossians 3:15-16a

***He** will keep in perfect peace **my** mind when **I** keep it steadfast, because I trust in **Him**.*
Isaiah 26:3

In peace I will lie down and sleep, for you alone, LORD, make me dwell in safety.
Psalm 4:8

My Place...

Do not fear, for He has Redeemed me; He has summoned me by name, I am His.
Isaiah 43:1b

*Since **I** am precious and honored in **His** sight, and because **He** loves **me**, **He** will give people in exchange for **me**, nations in exchange for **my** life. Do not be afraid, for **He** is with **me**.*
Isaiah 43:4-5a

*No one can deliver out of **His** hand. When **He** acts, who can reverse it?*
Isaiah 43:13b

*...for whoever touches **me**, touches the apple of his eye.*
Zechariah 2:8b

And we know that in all things God works for the good of those who love him, who have been called according to his purpose.
Romans 8:28

*Though **my** mother may forget **me**, **He** will not forget **me**! See, **He** has engraved **me** on the palms of **His** hands; my walls are ever before Him!*
Isaiah 49:16

*Remember these things...**He** made **me** and **I** am **His** servant. **He** will not forget **me**.*
Isaiah 44:21

*Yet you, LORD, are **my** Father. **I** am the clay, you are the potter; **I** am the work of your hand.*
Isaiah 64:8

Though my father and mother forsake me, the LORD will receive me.
Psalm 27:10

*Before **He** formed **me** in the womb **He** knew **me**, before **I** was born, **He** set **me** apart.*

Jeremiah 1:5

My Prayers...

If I have faith and do not doubt...If I believe, I will receive whatever I ask for in prayer.
Matthew 21:21-22

But blessed is the one who trusts in the LORD, whose confidence is in him.
Jeremiah 17:7

*I should confess **my** sins to others and pray for others so **I** may be healed. The prayer of a righteous person is powerful and effective.*
James 5:16

*When **I** call to **Him**, **He** will answer and tell **me** great and unsearchable things I do not know.*
Jeremiah 33:3

*Do not be anxious about anything, but in every situation, by prayer and petition, with thanksgiving, present **my** requests to God. And the peace of God, which transcends all understanding, will guard **my** heart and **my** mind in Christ Jesus.*
Philippians 4:6-7

I am your servant...whom you redeemed by your great strength and your mighty hand. Lord, let your ear be attentive to the prayer of this your servant and to the prayer of your servant who delights in revering your name.
Nehemiah 1:10-11

*I do not know what I ought to pray for, but the Spirit himself intercedes for **me** through wordless groans. And he who searches **my** heart knows the mind of the Spirit, because the Spirit intercedes for God's people in accordance with the will of God.*
Romans 8:26b-27

My Pride...

Who is wise and understanding among you? Let me show it by my good life, by deeds done in the humility that comes from wisdom.
James 3:13

"God opposes the proud but shows favor to the humble."
James 4:6b

*Humble **myself** before the Lord, he will lift **me** up.*
James 4:10

It looks down on all that are haughty; it is king over all that is proud.
Job 41:34

*Let someone else praise **me**, and not **my** own mouth; an outsider, and not **my** own lips.*
Proverbs 27:2

*Do not be arrogant, but tremble. For if God did not spare the natural branches, he will not spare **me** either.*
Romans 11:20b-21

*...Do not think of **myself** more highly than **I** ought, but rather think of **myself** with sober judgment, in accordance with the faith God has distributed to **me**.*
Romans 12:3

*My heart became proud on account of **my** beauty, and **I** corrupted **my** wisdom because of **my** splendor.*
Ezekiel 28:17

And those who walk in pride he is able to humble.
Daniel 4:37b

He saves the humble but bring low those who eyes are haughty.
Psalm 18:27

He guides the humble in what is right and teaches them his way.
Psalm 25:9

From their callous hearts comes iniquity; their evil imaginations have no limits.
Psalm 73:7

"But they, our ancestors, became arrogant and stiff-necked, and they did not obey your commands."
Nehemiah 9:16

*For who makes **me** different from anyone else? What do **I** have that **I** did not receive? And if **I** did receive it, why do **I** boast as though **I** did not?*
1 Corinthians 4:7

My Prison...

Set me free from my prison that I may praise your name.
Psalm 142:7a

Turn to me and be gracious to me, for I am lonely and afflicted.
Psalm 25:16

He lifted me out of the slimy pit, out of the mud and mire; he set my feet on a rock and gave me a firm place to stand.
Psalm 40:2

But the Lord is righteous; he has cut me free from the cords of the wicked.
Psalms 129:4

My Protection...

Guard my life and rescue me; do not let me be put to shame, for I take refuge in you. May integrity and uprightness protect me, because my hope, LORD, is in you.
Psalm 25:20-21

*Discretion will protect **me**, and understanding will guard **me**.*
Proverbs 2:11

Correction and instruction are the way to life.
Proverbs 6:23b

*Above all else, **I** need to guard **my** heart for everything **I** do flows from it.*
Proverbs 4:23

I have suffered much; preserve my life, LORD, according to your word.
Psalm 119:107

For your name's sake, LORD, preserve my life.
Psalm 143:11

*Because **I** love **Him**, **He** will rescue **me**; **He** will protect **me**, for **I** acknowledge **His** name.*
Psalm 91:14

***You** have put **your** words in **my** mouth and covered **me** with the shadow of **your** hand.*
Isaiah 51:16a

*For he will command his angels concerning **me** to guard **me** in all **my** ways.*
Psalm 91:11

***He** will do the very thing **I** have asked, because **He** is pleased with **me** and **He** knows **me** by name.*
Exodus 33:17

Though I walk in the midst of trouble, you preserve my life. You stretch out your hand against the anger of my foes; with your right hand you save me.
Psalm 138:7

My Purpose...

But the plans of the LORD stand firm forever, the purposes of his heart through all generations.
Psalm 33:11

*Before **He** formed **me** in the womb **He** knew **me**, before **I** was born **He** set **me** apart.*
Jeremiah 1:5

*For **He** knows the plans **He** has for **me**, plans to prosper **me** and not to harm **me**, plans to give **me** hope and a future.*
Jeremiah 29:11

*I must serve faithfully and wholeheartedly in the fear of the LORD. In every case that comes before **me**... I am to warn others not to sin against the LORD; otherwise his wrath will come on **me**. Do this, and I will not sin.*
2 Chronicles 19:9-10

The LORD will vindicate me; your love, LORD, endures forever - do not abandon the works of your hands.
Psalm 138:8

*Surely **He** will deliver **me** for a good purpose.*
Jeremiah 15:11a

For it is God who works in me to will and to act in order to fulfill his good purpose.
Philippians 2:13

Brothers and sisters, I do not consider myself yet to have taken hold of it. But one thing I do: Forgetting what is behind and straining toward what is ahead, I press on toward the goal to win the prize for which God has called me heavenward in Christ Jesus.
Philippians 3:13-14

The LORD Almighty has sworn, "Surely, as I have planned, so it will be, and as I have purposed, so it will happen." For the LORD Almighty has purposed, and who can thwart him? His hand is stretched out, and who can turn it back?
Isaiah 14:24, 27

My Refuge...

But whoever takes refuge in Him will inherit the land and possess His holy mountain.
Isaiah 57:13b

*For **I** died, and **my** life is now hidden with Christ in God.*
Colossians 3:3

But my eyes are fixed on you, Sovereign LORD; in you I take refuge - do not give me over to death.
Psalm 141:8

Show me the wonders of your great love, you who save by your right hand those who take refuge in you from their foes.
Psalm 17:7

The Lord is a refuge for the oppressed, a stronghold in times of trouble.
Psalm 9:9

My flesh and my heart may fail, but God is the strength of my heart and my portion forever. Those who are far from you will perish; you destroy all who are unfaithful to you. But as for me, it is good to be near God. I have made the Sovereign LORD my refuge; I will tell of all your deeds.
Psalm 73:26-28

My Relationships...

He has shown me, O mortal, what is good. And what does the LORD require of me? To act justly and to love mercy and to walk humbly with my God.
Micah 6:8

Blessed are the merciful, for they will be shown mercy.
Matthew 5:7

Turn from evil and do good; seek peace and pursue it. The eyes of the LORD are on the righteous, and his ears are attentive to their cry.
Psalm 34:14-15

A generous person will prosper; whoever refreshes others will be refreshed.
Proverbs 11:25

My Repentance...

Submit myself, then, to God. Resist the devil, and he will flee from me. Come near to God and he will come near to me. Wash my hands, sinner, and purify my heart for I am double-minded. Humble myself before the Lord, and he will lift me up.
James 4:7-8, 10

*Return to **Him** with all **my** heart, with fasting and weeping and mourning. Rend **my** heart and not **my** garments. Return to the LORD **my** God, for he is gracious and compassionate, slow to anger and abounding in love, and he relents from sending calamity.*
Joel 2:12-13

My sacrifice, O God, is a broken spirit; a broken and contrite heart you, God, will not despise.
Psalm 51:17

Yet you desired faithfulness even in the womb; you taught me wisdom in that secret place. Cleanse me with hyssop, and I will be clean; wash me, and I will be whiter than snow. Let me hear joy and gladness; let the bones you have crushed rejoice. Hide your face from my sins and blot out all my iniquity. Create in me a pure heart, O God, and renew a steadfast spirit within me.
Psalm 51:6-10

Then I acknowledged my sin to you and did not cover up my iniquity. I said, "I will confess my transgressions to the LORD." And you forgave the guilt of my sin.
Psalm 32:5

Do not remember the sins of my youth and my rebellious ways; according to your love remember me, for you, LORD, are good.
Psalm 25:7

For the sake of your name, LORD, forgive my iniquity, though it is great.
Psalm 25:11

My Repentance...
For I am about to fall, and my pain is ever with me. I confess my iniquity; I am troubled by my sin.
Psalm 38:17-18

But who can discern their own errors? Forgive my hidden faults. Keep your servant also from willful sins; may they not rule over me. Then I will be blameless, innocent of great transgression.
Psalm 19:12-13

My Safety...

You, LORD, will keep the needy safe and will protect me forever from the wicked.
Psalm 12:7

Keep me safe, my God, for in you I take refuge.
Psalm 16:1

He reached down from on high and took hold of me; he drew me out of deep waters. He rescued me from my powerful enemy, from my foes, who were too strong for me. They confronted me in the day of my disaster, but the Lord was my support. He brought me out into a spacious place; he rescued me because he delighted in me.
Psalm 18:16-19

I will continue to rejoice, for I know that through your prayers and God's provision of the Spirit of Jesus Christ what has happened to me will turn out for my deliverance.
Philippians 1:18b-19

My Sin...

I must consecrate myself, for tomorrow the LORD will do amazing things!
Joshua 3:5

*He will deal with **me** according to **my** conduct, and by **my** own standards **He** will judge **me**. Then **I** will know the **He** is the Lord.*
Ezekiel 7:27b

*My wickedness with punish **me**; **my** backsliding will rebuke **me**. Consider then and realize how evil and bitter it is for me when **I** forsake the Lord **my** God and have no awe of Him.*
Jeremiah 2:19

The fruit of righteousness will be peace. The effect of righteousness will be quietness and confidence forever.
Isaiah 32:17

*If **I** repent, **He** will restore **me** that **I** may serve **Him**; if **I** utter worthy, not worthless, words, **I** will be **His** spokesman.*
Jeremiah 15:19

Renounce your sins by doing what is right, and your wickedness by being kind to the oppressed. It may be that then your prosperity will continue.
Daniel 4:27

"I, the LORD, search the heart and examine the mind, to reward each person according to their conduct, according to what their deeds deserve."
Jeremiah 17:10

But who can discern their own errors? Forgive my hidden faults. Keep your servant also from willful sins; may they not rule over me. Then I will be blameless, innocent of great transgression. May these words of my mouth and this meditation of my heart be pleasing in your sight, LORD, my Rock and my Redeemer.
Psalm 19:12-13

My Strength...

Woe to those who...rely on horses, who trust in the multitude of their chariots and in the great strength of their horsemen, but do not look to the Holy One of Israel, or seek help from the LORD.
Isaiah 31:1

*Has **He** not commanded **me**? Be strong and courageous. Do not be afraid; do not be discouraged, for the LORD **my** God will be wherever I go.*
Joshua 1:9

...for the joy of the LORD is your strength!
Nehemiah 8:10b

*So do not fear, for **He** is with **me**; do not be dismayed for **He** is **my** God. **He** will strengthen **me** and help **me**. **He** will uphold **me** with **His** righteous right hand.*
Isaiah 41:10

*When **I** hope in the LORD **my** strength will be renewed. **I** will soar on wings like eagles; **I** will run and not grow weary, **I** will walk and not be faint.*
Isaiah 40:31

I love you, LORD, my strength. The LORD is my rock, my fortress and my deliverer; my God is my rock, in whom I take refuge, my shield and the horn of my salvation, my stronghold.
Psalm 18:1-2

My soul is weary with sorrow; strengthen me according to your word.
Keep me from deceitful ways; be gracious to me through your law.
Psalm 119:28-29

The Sovereign LORD is my strength; he makes my feet like the feet of a
deer, he enables me to tread on the heights.
Habakkuk 3:19

My Transformation...

In order to be transformed by His power, I must acknowledge and
take to heart the Lord is God of heaven and earth! He is all powerful
and His strength will overcome any and all obstacles, life's circumstances, people's choices, or my pain. His power is stronger than all
of it!

~Diane Pearce

Acknowledge and take to heart this day that the LORD is God in heaven
above and on the earth below. There is no other.
Deuteronomy 4:39

And we all, who with unveiled face contemplate the Lord's glory, are be-
ing transformed into his image with ever-increasing glory which comes
from the Lord, who is the Spirit.
 2 Corinthians 3:18

Do not conform to the pattern of this world, but be transformed by the
renewing of my mind.
Romans 12:2

*The LORD did not set his affection on **me** and choose **me** because **I** was more numerous than other people, for **I** was the fewest of all people. But it was because the LORD loved **me** and kept the oath he swore to **my** ancestors that he brought **me** out with a mighty hand and redeemed **me** from the land of slavery.*
Deuteronomy 7:7-8

*LORD, there is no one like you to help the powerless against the mighty. Help **me**, LORD my God, for **I** rely on you, and in your name **I** have come against this vast army. LORD, you are **my** God; do not let mere mortals prevail against you.*
2 Chronicles 14:11

My Trust...

I will trust in the LORD with all my heart and lean on my own understanding; in all my ways submit to him, and he will make my path straight.
Proverbs 3:5-6

But I trust in your unfailing love; my heart rejoices in your salvation.
Psalm 13:5

Keep me safe, my God, for in you I take refuge.
Psalm 16:1

When they hurled their insults at him, he did not retaliate; when he suffered, he made no threats. Instead, he entrusted himself to him who judges justly.
1 Peter 2:23

The name of the Lord is a fortified tower; the righteous run to it and are safe.
Proverbs 18:10

Many seek an audience with a ruler, but it is from the Lord that one gets justice.
Proverbs 29:26

The Lord is good to those whose hope is in him, to the one who seeks him.
Lamentations 3:25

My Victory...

It was not by my sword that I won the land, nor did my arm bring me victory; it was your right hand, your arm, and the light of your face, for you loved me.
Psalm 44:3

*Do not be afraid or discouraged because of this vast army. For the battle is not **mine**, but God's...**I** will not have to fight this battle. **I** will take up **my** position; stand firm and see the deliverance the LORD will give **me**...Do not be afraid; do not be discouraged. I will go out to face them tomorrow, and the Lord will be with **me**.*
2 Chronicles 20:15-17

You make your saving help my shield, and your right hand sustains me; your help has made me great.
Psalm 18:35

I put no trust in my bow, my sword does not bring me victory; but you give us victory over our enemies, you put our adversaries to shame.
Psalm 44:6-7

My Waiting...

No eye has seen any God besides you, who acts on behalf of those who wait for him.
Isaiah 64:4b

In the time of your favor...answer me.
Psalm 69:13

Be joyful in hope, patient in affliction, faithful in prayer. Share with the Lord's people who are in need. Practice hospitality! Bless those who persecute you!
Romans 12:12-14

Yet the LORD longs to be gracious to **me***; therefore he will rise up to show* **me** *compassion. For the LORD is a God of justice. Blessed am* **I** *when* **I** *wait for him!*
Isaiah 30:18

I remain confident of this: I will see the goodness of the LORD in the land of the living. Wait for the LORD; be strong and take heart and wait for the LORD.
Psalm 27:13-14

I heard and my heart pounded, my lips quivered at the sound; decay crept into my bones, and my legs trembled. Yet I will wait patiently for the day of calamity to come on the nation invading us. Though the fig tree does not bud and there are no grapes on the vines, though the olive crop fails and the fields produce no food, though there are no sheep in the pen and no cattle in the stalls, yet I will rejoice in the LORD, I will be joyful in God my Savior. The Sovereign LORD is my strength; he makes my feet like the feet of a deer, he enables me to tread on the heights.
Habakkuk 3:16-19

My Walk...

Know that the LORD is God! It is he who made me, and I am his. I am his people, a sheep of his pasture!
Psalm 100:3

Enter His gates with thanksgiving and his courts with praise; give thanks to him and praise his name. For the LORD is good and his love endures forever; his faithfulness continues through all generations.
Psalm 100:4-5

It is God who arms me with strength and keeps my way secure. He makes my feet like the feet of a deer; he causes me to stand on the heights.
Psalm 18:32-33

He refreshes my soul. He guides me along the right paths for his name's sake. Even though I walk through the darkest valley, I will fear no evil, for you are with me; your rod and your staff, they comfort me.
Psalm 23:3-4

My Wisdom...

But the wisdom that comes from heaven is first pure; then peace-loving, considerate, submissive, full of mercy and good fruit, impartial and sincere.
James 3:17

Therefore everyone who hears these words of mine and puts them into practice is like a wise man who built his house on the rock.
Matthew 7:24

The prudent see danger and take refuge, but the simple keep going and pay the penalty. If anyone loudly blesses their neighbor early in the morning, it will be taken as a curse. A quarrelsome wife is like the dripping of a leaky roof in a rainstorm.
Proverbs 27:12, 14-15

If I lack wisdom, I should ask God, who gives generously to all without finding fault, and it will be given to me.
James 1:5

And this is my prayer: that your love may abound more and more in knowledge and depth of insight, so that you may be able to discern what is best and may be pure and blameless for the day of Christ, filled with the fruit of righteousness that comes through Jesus Christ—to the glory and praise of God.
Philippians 1:9-11

I am your servant; give me discernment that I may understand your statutes.
Psalm 119:125

My son, do not let wisdom and understanding out of your sight, preserve sound judgment and discretion.
Proverbs 3:21

The law of the Lord is perfect, refreshing the soul. The statutes of the Lord are trustworthy, making wise the simple. The precepts of the Lord are right, giving joy to the heart. The commands of the Lord are radiant, giving light to the eyes.
Psalm 19:7-8

The mouths of the righteous utter wisdom, and their tongues speak what is just.
Psalm 37:30

Yet you desired faithfulness even in the womb; you taught me wisdom in that secret place.
Psalm 51:6

My Work...

The LORD will vindicate me; your love, LORD, endures forever - do not abandon the works of your hands.
Psalm 138:8

"Not by might nor by power, but by my spirit", says the Lord Almighty!
Zechariah 4:6b

Do not be afraid, but let your hands by strong!
Zechariah 8:13b

*I will fight because the LORD is with **me**, and **I** will put the enemy... to shame.*
Zechariah 10:5b

__You__ bring __me__ back from captivity... so __I__ may bring __you__ renown, joy, praise and honor.
Jeremiah 33:7a, 9a

*Whatever **I** do, **I** need to work at it with all **my** heart, as working for the Lord, not for human masters, since **I** know that **I** will receive an inheritance from the Lord as a reward. It is the Lord Christ **I** am serving.*
Colossians 3:23-24

Produce fruit in keeping with repentance.
Matthew 3:8

My Worship...

If I follow worthless idols, I will become a worthless idol myself.
Jeremiah 2:5b

Come, let us sing for joy to the Lord; let us shout aloud to the Rock of our salvation. Let us come before him with thanksgiving and extol him with music and song.
Psalm 95:1-2

Come, let us bow down in worship, let us kneel before the Lord our Maker; for he is our God and we are the people of his pasture, the flock under his care.
Psalm 95:6-7

My Wounds...

But He will restore me to health and heal my wounds...because I am called an outcast.
Jeremiah 30:17

The LORD is close to the brokenhearted and saves those who are crushed in spirit.
Psalm 34:18

My heart pounds, my strength fails me; even the light has gone from my eyes. My friends and companions avoid me because of my wounds; my neighbors stay far away.
Psalm 38:10-11

Set me free from my prison, that I may praise your name. Then the righteous will gather about me because of your goodness to me.
Psalm 142:7

Provide for those who grieve in Zion—to bestow on them a crown of beauty instead of ashes, the oil of joy instead of mourning, and a garment of praise instead of a spirit of despair. They will be called oaks of righteousness, a planting of the Lord for the display of his splendor.
Isaiah 61:3

You intended to harm me, but God intended it for good to accomplish what is now being done, the saving of many lives.
Genesis 50:20

~notes~

~notes~

About the Author

M. Diane Pearce, Ph.D., LMFT (Licensed Marriage and Family Therapist), is the Founder and Director of Legacy Strategy, Inc., a biblically based counseling practice located in Kennesaw, Georgia. Connect with her at www.legacystrategy.com and on Twitter @DianePearce1.

Diane has provided counseling full time in a private practice setting since 1984. She became licensed after receiving her Masters in Marriage, Family & Child Counseling from the Rosemead School of Psychology at Biola University in 1984. After practicing as a Licensed Marriage and Family therapist, she earned her Ph.D. in Family Mediation from LaSalle University in 1998. She counsels individuals, married couples, and families and does so with a practical and passionate approach so her clients may have the most positive impact possible on others. Diane specializes in relationship and marriage issues, including affair prevention and recovery. In addition, she treats those with depression, anxiety, abuse recovery, attachment difficulties, dissociation, trauma, and eating disorders.

Diane has done extensive radio work including co-hosting the "Marriage and Family Today" radio show on WAFS AM 920 (Moody Radio in Atlanta, GA) and "A Woman's Perspective" on WAFG 90.3 (Ft. Lauderdale, FL). She currently serves as adjunct faculty at Liberty University in Lynchburg Virginia and as Clinical Supervisor to Graduate Students at Richmont University in Atlanta, Georgia. In addition, she has been a Fellow with the American Association of Marriage and Family Therapy since 1984 and Clinical Supervisor with them since

2011. She is also a member of the American Association of Christian Counselors, and the Christian Association of Psychological Studies.

But mostly, Diane enjoys being a wife and mother who is passionate about leaving a legacy of her own as well as equipping others with the tools that are necessary for them to leave a divinely appointed legacy.

59260867R00084

Made in the USA
Charleston, SC
31 July 2016